THAT'S CUTE, YOU'RE 18: NOW IT'S TIME TO BUCKLE UP!

Girl Edition

"*That's Cute, You're 18! Now It's Time to Buckle Up!*" is the ultimate go-to guide for every 18-year-old girl, packed with quirky and entertaining advice on navigating the rollercoaster of adulthood. From managing friendships, relationships, and heartbreak to conquering the challenges of menstrual cycles, managing money, and even understanding US voting, this book covers it all. With a playful tone and relatable insights, it empowers young women to embrace their independence, tackle life's ups and downs, prioritize mental health, and make informed decisions. Get ready to buckle up and embark on an exciting journey of self-discovery, growth, and success in the on-going journey that we all call adulthood.

By
Riley B Jordan

Copyright 2023 - Riley B Jordan - All Rights Reserved.

Unauthorized reproduction of this book, in whole or in part, is strictly prohibited. This includes any form of duplication, distribution, or transmission without the explicit written permission of the author, Riley B Jordan.

For requests, please contact the author: rileybjordanbooks@outlook.com

CONTENTS

Introduction 1

Chapter 1: Welcome To Adulthood!
The 18th Birthday Blues: Confronting Expectations 5
Your Identity Isn't Carved in Stone: Navigating Change 8
Free to Be: Defining Independence 11

Chapter 2: Friends: The Spice of Life
The Joy and Pain of Friendship: Ups and Downs 15
Choosing the Right Friends: Quality over Quantity 18
From Besties to Frenemies: Handling Conflict 20

Chapter 3: Love, Lust, and Everything In-Between
First Love and Heartbreak: The Rollercoaster of Emotions .. 24
Love vs Lust: Deciphering Feelings 27
The Art of Healthy Boundaries in Relationships 30
Breaking Up Like A Pro 33
"Is He Flirting With Me?" 36

Chapter 4: The Crimson Wave: Making Peace with Your Period

From Embarrassment to Acceptance: Dealing with Period Stigma **40**
Mastering Your Cycle: Tips and Tricks **43**
Your Body, Your Rules: Feminine Hygiene Myths Debunked . **46**

Chapter 5: Money Matters: Dollars and Sense
Earning, Saving, Spending, Budgeting: Managing Your First Paychecks **50**
Budgeting: The Not-So-Fun but Oh-So-Crucial Game **53**
Credit Cards, Loans, and Debts: The Financial Spice Rack ... **56**
Investing for Your Future: Money Grows on Trees...Sort Of .. **59**

Chapter 6: The Big "M": Considering Marriage
From Hollywood to Reality: Demystifying Marriage **62**
When It's Right, It's Right: Timing and Marriage **64**
Single and Loving It: You Don't Have to Say 'I Do' **66**

Chapter 7: Voting: The Power Is in Your Hands
The Importance of Your Vote: Every Voice Matters **69**
Navigating the Political Landscape: Parties, Policies, etc **71**
Voting Made Easy: Demystifying the Process **73**

Chapter 8: Mental Health: It's Okay to Not Be Okay
The Silent Battle: Understanding Mental Health **76**
Self-Care Isn't Selfish: Building Healthy Habits **79**
Just Feeling Blue or is it Something More? Understanding the Difference **82**
Getting Help: Therapy and Beyond **85**

Chapter 9: College or Not: Making the Big Decision
University 101: The Pros and Cons **89**
Exploring Alternatives: Trade Schools, Gap Years, etc **91**
Surviving the Pressure: Choosing What's Best for You **93**

Chapter 10: Body Image: Embracing the Skin You're In
The Mirror Lies: Confronting Body Dysmorphia **96**
Health vs Size: Understanding the Difference **98**
Celebrating You: Tips for Positive Body Image **101**
Building a Supportive Community: Surrounding Yourself with Positive Influences **104**
Self-Care and Body Positivity: Practicing Love and Acceptance **107**

Chapter 11: Social Media: Friend or Foe?
The Highlight Reel: Understanding the Illusion **111**
Social Media Detox: Taking Time Off **114**
Creating a Positive Online Presence **117**

Chapter 12: Sexual Health: More Than Just the "Talk"
The Birds, Bees, and Everything In-Between: Safe Sex Education **121**
Consent is Sexy: Understanding Boundaries **124**
STDs, Screenings, and Prevention: Keeping It Safe **127**
Healthy Relationships and Communication: Nurturing Intimacy **130**
Exploring Your Sexual Identity: Embracing Diversity and Self-Discovery **133**

Mental and Emotional Well-being:
Addressing the Psychological Aspects of Sexual Health **136**

Chapter 13: Career Planning:
Chase the Dream, Not the Money

Finding Your Passion: The Job vs Career Debate **140**
Internships, Resumes, and Interviews: The Basics **142**
The Hustle: Managing Stress in the Workplace **144**

Chapter 14: Adulting 101:
The Stuff They Don't Teach You

Bills, Taxes, and Insurance: The Basics **147**
Cooking, Cleaning, Laundry:
Domestic Goddesses in the Making **150**
Time Management: Work, Life, and Play **153**

Chapter 15: Substance Use: Knowing the Risks

Alcohol and Drugs: The Reality Beyond the Party **157**
Understanding Addiction: When Fun Becomes Fatal **160**
Help and Support: Recovery is Possible **163**
Peer Pressure and Saying No: Navigating Social Situations .. **166**

Chapter 16: Relationships with Parents:
The Evolving Bond

From Dependence to Independence: Shifting Dynamics **170**
Setting Boundaries with Parents: Navigating Disagreements **173**
Appreciating Family: The Importance of Gratitude **176**

Chapter 17: Self-Exploration: Discovering Your True Potential

Embracing Your Passions: Unleashing Your Creative Side .. **180**
Setting Goals and Dreaming Big:
Turning Ambitions into Reality **183**
Exploring Your Strengths and Weaknesses:
Understanding Your Potential **186**
Facing Fears: Stepping Out of Your Comfort Zone **189**
Self-Reflection and Growth:
The Power of Personal Development **192**
Finding Your Purpose:
Aligning Your Passions with a Meaningful Path **195**

Chapter 18: Cultivating Resilience: Bouncing Back from Life's Challenges

The Power of Resilience: Building Inner Strength **199**
Coping with Failure and Rejection:
Turning Setbacks into Opportunities **202**
Mindset Shift: Embracing a Positive Attitude **205**
Managing Stress and Overwhelm: Strategies for Well-being .. **208**
Building a Support System: Nurturing Healthy Relationships . **211**
Thriving Through Adversity:
Embracing Change and Adaptability **214**

Conclusion **217**

INTRODUCTION

"Embrace the Chaos, Girl!"

Oh, hey there, you amazing, fierce, and slightly overwhelmed 18-year-old girl! Congratulations on stepping into the exhilarating world of adulthood. *Cue confetti cannons and a chorus of off-key singing* (we can't provide the singing bit in this book, maybe ask your mom and dad). Welcome to a journey that's about to throw you headfirst into a whirlwind of excitement, challenges, and countless "what-the-hell-was-I-thinking" moments. Buckle up, my friend, because life just pressed the turbo button, and you're in for one hell of a ride!

You might be thinking, "What the heck am I supposed to do now?" Take a deep breath, my dear, and let me tell you a little secret: none of us really know what we're doing either! But that's part of the magic. Life isn't a perfectly scripted sitcom or a meticulously planned itinerary. It's more like a wild roller coaster that takes unexpected turns, makes you scream, laugh, and sometimes puke (figuratively speaking, of course). In this book, we're going to dive headlong into the nitty-gritty of being 18, a time of epic self-discovery, heartbreak, and figuring out how to adult without adulting too hard. We'll chat about friendships that will shape you, relationships that will confuse you, and heartbreaks that will make you want to eat ice cream directly from the tub. We'll explore the mysterious world of menstrual cycles—yeah, it's not all roses and rainbows, but hey, knowledge is power!

But wait, there's more! We won't just be diving into your personal life. We're also going to talk about managing that hard-earned cash (cue visions of shopping sprees and late-night pizza deliveries), navigating the treacherous terrain of marriage (or maybe just the idea of it), and even tackling the wild world of U.S. voting, because being a badass citizen is essential!

Now, let's be real for a sec. Life isn't always sunshine and rainbows. It can be a tough cookie to crack, and sometimes it feels like the universe is testing you with every conceivable challenge. That's why we'll delve into the depths of mental health, helping you build resilience and reminding you that it's perfectly okay to seek help when the going gets tough. We're here for all the ups, downs, sideways, and loop-de-loops life throws at you.

Throughout this journey, we're going to laugh, because let's face it, humor is the ultimate life hack. We're going to get real, because vulnerability is our superpower. And we're going to celebrate your unique, beautiful, and badass self, because you, my dear, are the protagonist of your story.

So, grab your favorite beverage, find a cozy nook, and get ready to embark on a roller coaster ride called adulthood. This book is your survival guide, your cheerleader, and your comrade-in-arms. Together, we'll tackle the challenges, embrace the triumphs, and navigate the intricacies of this crazy, wonderful thing we call life.

Are you ready? I sure hope so! Buckle up, hold on tight, and unleash the unstoppable force within you. Oh, wow! You're 18! Let the adventure begin!

and so the ADVENTURE begins

CHAPTER 1:

WELCOME TO ADULTHOOD

The 18th Birthday Blues: Confronting Expectations

Turning 18 is often hyped up as the grand entrance into adulthood. It's like everyone expects you to wake up on your 18th birthday, suddenly wearing that elegant cloak of responsibility and maturity. Instead, you probably felt like you were trying to navigate through a Halloween party dressed in a clashing ensemble of adult responsibilities and teenage insecurities, all while wearing oversized shoes of expectation that keep making you trip.

One day you're furiously Googling whether a group of unicorns is called a blessing or a sparkle (it's a blessing, by the way), and the next, you're supposed to be an 'adult.' Suddenly, you're expected to make life-changing decisions, know how to vote, and perhaps most intimidating of all, cook something other than instant ramen or toast without causing a minor kitchen fire.

You know that daunting moment when you open an IKEA flat-pack furniture box, and it's just a million pieces with a tiny wrench and a cryptic manual that might as well be ancient hieroglyphics? Of course not, you've never done that before, have you? That's what stepping into adulthood feels like.

Let me tell you, it's entirely okay if you didn't wake up on your 18th birthday feeling all grown-up and wise. Heck, it's okay if you still enjoy watching Saturday morning cartoons while eating Fruity Pebbles instead of reading the financial news over a balanced protein smoothie. Real talk: any adult who says they don't occasionally indulge in a bowl of sugary cereal is probably a robot– or worse, they might be lying to you.

Turning 18 can feel like a heavy weight because it comes with many expectations. Society expects you to know your life path, to have a concrete plan, to know how to deal with the IRS, and, somehow, also to master the art of 'light' laundry loads versus 'heavy' loads. Newsflash: your white clothes don't have to become victims of that rogue red sock every time.

But here's a secret, wrapped up and handed to you on a silver platter: It's okay if you don't have all of this figured out yet. The adults you see around you? They're just oversized kids in disguise who are winging it and learning on the go. Adulthood isn't a magic portal you step through when the clock strikes midnight on your 18th birthday. It's not a Cinderella story; there's no fairy godmother who'll wave her wand and transform you into a grown-up with all the knowledge about credit scores and tax brackets.

Your 18th birthday isn't a deadline; it's the starting line of a marathon. The road ahead is long and winding, filled with uphill struggles, downhill sprints, refreshing water breaks, and yes, even some scraped knees. Adulthood isn't about knowing everything; it's about learning, growing, and being resilient enough to keep moving forward.

Confront those expectations head-on and understand that they are often societal pressures, not realities. Toss aside the 'shoulds'– the things you think you should be doing or should know. Embrace the 'coulds'–the opportunities for exploration, the freedom to learn, to make mistakes, and to find your unique path. This is your marathon, your journey. You're not competing with anyone else.

Remember, 18 is just a number. It doesn't define your worth or your abilities. This year is your first step into the vast, sometimes bewildering, but always thrilling journey of adulthood. So, buckle up and enjoy the ride. Your 18th year isn't about having all the answers; it's about starting to ask the right questions and discovering who you want to become. You've got this, and remember: unicorns would totally rock at this adulting thing too.

Your Identity Isn't Carved in Stone: Navigating Change

Now that we've hopefully made it clear that turning 18 doesn't come with a magical upgrade in life skills or a manual titled "How to Adult 101," let's dive into another biggie: your identity. You've probably spent the last few years working out who you are, like a jigsaw puzzle where the pieces keep changing shapes, and you're unsure of the picture you're trying to create.

One day, you're entirely convinced you're an introverted cat-person who's going to write the next great American novel. The next, you find yourself dreaming about life on the road as a traveling DJ with a pet iguana. While this might seem confusing, it's actually entirely normal. Your identity isn't a sculpture chiseled in marble; it's more like a masterpiece painted in watercolors, constantly blending, bleeding, and transforming into something new and beautiful.

Turning 18 comes with its fair share of identity crises. People will start expecting you to have a solid, well-detailed life plan. When someone asks, "What do you want to do with your life?" or "What's your five-year plan?" it feels like they're demanding you carve your identity into stone right there and then. I mean, how are you supposed to answer that? "Well, in five years, I plan to have binge-watched at least ten more Netflix series, mastered the art of folding a fitted sheet, and discovered a foolproof method for picking the fastest checkout line at the supermarket." Sounds like a solid plan, right?

Society tends to create a narrative that we must have our lives all figured out by the time we hit 18. That we should know exactly who we are, what we want, and how we're going to get it. But hey, who set these rules? You're not a fortune cookie; you can't just crack open and have all the answers neatly written out.

The truth is, it's perfectly okay, even advantageous, to allow your identity to evolve and change. You're not the same person you were when you were 15, and you probably won't be the exact same person at 25, or 35, or 45. Life is about exploration, learning, growing, making mistakes, and then learning some more.

Adulthood doesn't mean you suddenly stop exploring who you are. It's not a stop sign, it's a green light, signaling you to keep moving, keep exploring, keep evolving. You're allowed to change your mind, to pivot, to find new passions, and let go of old ones. You're allowed to be a lover of romantic comedies today and a horror aficionado tomorrow. You're allowed to love sushi this week and detest it the next.

You're allowed to dress in all black one day and rock a neon pink tutu the next. You're allowed to be a badass boss babe one moment and a vulnerable human the next. Your identity isn't a one-size-fits-all; it's custom-made by you, for you, and it can change as you do.

Being 18 and stepping into adulthood means you have the beautiful opportunity to continue discovering who you are, with the added bonus of a little more freedom and a lot more experiences. Remember, the aim isn't to carve your identity into a block of unchangeable stone but to paint a unique masterpiece that represents you in all your evolving glory.

And remember, just like any great work of art, it's never truly finished; it continues to evolve and transform. Embrace the uncertainty, and remember to enjoy the process. After all, a wise philosopher (or was it a meme on Instagram?) once said, "Life isn't about finding yourself; it's about creating yourself."

Create

Free to Be:
Defining Independence

And so, we've arrived at the bustling city of Independence, a metropolis in the world of adulthood that is just as terrifying as it is exciting. Independence. It's a word that has been on your lips and in your dreams, like a mythical unicorn, glittering with promise and freedom. And now that you're 18, independence is not just a far-off dream—it's a reality.

You know that exhilarating feeling when you're at the top of a rollercoaster, right before the drop? That's what 18 feels like. You're on top of the world with a newfound independence, but the plunge into the journey of self-reliance can be equally exhilarating and intimidating.

We often equate independence with big, bold things like moving out, starting college, getting a job, or learning how to cook something that doesn't involve the words "instant" or "microwaveable." But the truth is, independence isn't just about these large, monumental shifts. It's also about the small but significant choices you make every day.

Think of independence as a newly acquired superpower. You remember how Peter Parker handled his newfound spider abilities (after a few awkward mishaps, of course)? Yeah, it's kind of like that, but minus the spandex suit and the whole web-slinging business (unless that's what you're into, then, by all means, sling away!).

As Uncle Ben wisely said, "With great power comes great responsibility." Your new superpower of independence means you have the freedom to make choices. It means deciding what you want to eat for dinner without having a family vote or choosing the movie for movie night without having to compromise for your little brother's obsession with animated talking cars.

But it also means taking responsibility for those choices. It means learning to budget your money so you don't end up subsisting on instant noodles for the last week of every month. It means dealing with the consequences when you decide to procrastinate and binge-watch that new Netflix series instead of studying for your test.

Defining your independence will look different for everyone. It might mean booking your own doctor's appointments, balancing your checkbook, or tackling the daunting pile of laundry that you've sworn is starting to develop its own ecosystem. It's making your own choices, standing up for what you believe in, and learning to trust yourself.

Being independent doesn't mean you have to do everything alone. It's not about never asking for help or advice. Everyone needs a helping hand or a listening ear sometimes, and asking for help when you need it is actually a sign of strength and maturity.

In the grand adventure of independence, remember to be patient with yourself. You'll stumble, you'll fall, and there might be a few wrong turns or detours along the way. But that's part of the journey. Each mistake is an opportunity to learn and grow.

So here you are, standing at the edge of the thrilling drop of your roller coaster ride, armed with your superpower of independence. Embrace it, enjoy it, and remember that it's okay to throw your hands up in the air and scream sometimes. After all, that's part of the fun of roller coasters—and of independence. Just remember to hold on tight, keep your eyes open, and enjoy the ride. The view from the top is just the beginning!

Chapter 2:

FRIENDS: THE SPICE OF LIFE

The Joy and Pain of Friendship: Ups and Downs

Ah, friendships. They're like a bowl of spicy salsa–sweet, tangy, a little bit fiery, and oh-so-necessary for a well-rounded life (or taco). Just like that jalapeno-laden salsa, friendships can give you a bout of joyous giggles or make your eyes water with a sting. Friendships, especially when you're navigating the tumultuous waters of young adulthood, can be as complicated as trying to solve a Rubik's cube in the dark.

As you step into your 18th year, friendships can start to feel like a game of human Tetris. You're constantly moving, growing, and shifting, and so are your friends. And sometimes, just as you think you've found the perfect fit, the shapes change, and you're left trying to figure out where the pieces go.

On one hand, friendships can be as comforting as a warm mug of hot chocolate on a chilly day. A good friend is like a human diary, someone who knows your history and doesn't need an explanation about that time you dyed your hair green on a dare or why you can't stand the smell of burnt popcorn.

They're the ones who know your Instagram poses, who "oooh" and "aaah" at the right time when you're telling a story, and who know the exact kind of weird memes that will make you laugh until your stomach hurts. They're the ones you can sit with in comfortable silence or have deep conversations about life, the universe, and the latest celebrity drama.

On the other hand, friendships can sometimes feel like walking through a cactus garden—mostly beautiful but occasionally prickly and painful. Disagreements can flare up hotter than a forgotten pizza in the oven, misunderstandings can create chasms wider than your desire to re-watch your favorite show, and sometimes, friendships can fade away, leaving you with a nostalgic ache.

Remember that movie you loved as a kid, but when you rewatched it as a teen, you realized it didn't hold the same magic? That's okay. The same goes for friendships. As you grow, some friendships might not grow with you. People change, and sometimes, that means drifting apart. That doesn't take away from the beautiful friendship you had; it just means that it served its purpose in its time.

Navigating the ups and downs of friendships at 18 means learning to communicate, understanding that disagreements don't mean disloyalty, and realizing it's okay to let go of friendships that no longer serve you.

In the roller coaster ride of friendship, remember to hold on to the safety bar of respect and communication, enjoy the exciting loops of shared experiences and joy, and brace yourself for the inevitable drops of disagreement and misunderstanding.

And always remember: Just as salsa wouldn't be the same without a bit of spice, life wouldn't be the same without a bit of friendship drama. It's the blend of sweet, sour, and spicy moments that make friendships so incredibly special and worthwhile. So, buckle up, keep an open mind, and prepare for the thrilling ride that is friendship at 18. After all, even a roller coaster ride is dull without its ups and downs.

Choosing the Right Friends: Quality over Quantity

The journey of friendship is a bit like shopping at a thrift store. Sometimes you have to sift through a heap of ill-fitting, mothball-scented sweaters to find that perfect vintage jacket that seems like it was made just for you. It's not about how many clothes you try on; it's about finding those perfect pieces that make you feel like a million bucks (or at least a very confident 18-year-old).

It's the same with friendships. In your lifetime, you'll meet hundreds, maybe even thousands, of people. But not everyone you meet will become your friend, and that's okay. The goal isn't to collect friends like Pokemon cards, where you're trying to amass a vast quantity. Instead, it's about quality. It's about finding those friends who get you, who support you, and who make you feel good about yourself.

Choosing the right friends isn't about finding people who are exactly like you. It's not about finding someone who agrees with you all the time, loves the same bands, and hates the same foods. Real friends aren't "yes" people. They're the ones who will tell you when you're going down a wrong path or when that neon green eyeshadow really isn't your color.

True friends are a bit like that vintage jacket you found at the thrift store - they may not be perfect, and they might come with their own unique quirks and idiosyncrasies. But they fit you perfectly. They celebrate your successes, pick you up when you fall, and are there for you, even when the chips are down.

But how do you choose these magical unicorn friends? It's not like they come with labels, right?

Look for friends who treat you with kindness and respect, who listen when you talk and value your opinion. Good friends won't try to change you into someone you're not, and they won't make you feel small or insignificant. They'll encourage your dreams, laugh at your jokes (even the bad ones), and be there for you, even when it's not convenient for them.

Remember, the size of your friend group doesn't define your worth or popularity. It's not a numbers game. Having a handful of close, meaningful friendships is infinitely better than having an army of acquaintances.

In the end, choosing the right friends is about recognizing the value they add to your life and the value you add to theirs. It's about cherishing the friendships that lift you up, make you laugh, and enrich your life. It's about quality over quantity every time. After all, who needs a closet full of ill-fitting sweaters when you've got that perfect vintage jacket?

From Besties to Frenemies: Handling Conflict

Let's dive into a scenario that we all know too well. You've just made yourself a big bowl of popcorn, sprinkled some of that ridiculously addictive cheddar seasoning on it, settled in your favorite comfy spot, and are about to binge-watch the latest season of your guilty-pleasure reality show when your phone buzzes. It's your bestie, and she's mad. Something about you, her, and a tweet that was apparently a subtweet that led to a mega misunderstanding. Suddenly, you're not binge-watching; you're damage controlling.

Welcome to the realm of friendship conflicts, where the weather forecast often includes stormy emotions with a chance of flying accusations. Just as a mighty oak tree can't grow without a few storms, a solid friendship often weathers its share of conflicts. So, how do we handle these friendship squalls without losing our besties or our sanity? Buckle up, and let's navigate these stormy seas together.

The first thing to remember when dealing with conflict is to breathe. Not just because you need oxygen to live, but because taking a moment to calm down can help you approach the situation with a clearer head. Rushing in with your emotions on your sleeve may lead to you saying things you might regret. And no, you can't use the "I was just mad" card to take them back.

Words are like confetti; once they're out there, you can't put them back in the bag.

Communication is your compass in the storm. We often assume that our friends can read our minds, understand our cryptic texts, or decode our subtweets. Spoiler alert: They can't. And to be honest, if they could, that would be terrifying. Be open about your feelings without launching accusations. You know the drill, stick to "I" statements. Instead of saying, "You never listen to me," try, "I feel ignored when I'm talking to you."

Remember that conflicts aren't about winning or losing. It's not a wrestling match (unless you and your friend are actually into wrestling, in which case, cool!). The aim is to resolve the issue, not score points. Sometimes, this means agreeing to disagree. At other times, it may mean compromise. Swallowing your pride might seem as pleasant as swallowing a cactus, but trust me, it's less prickly in the long run.

Apologizing is an art, a beautifully humbling art. If you're wrong, own it. A sincere apology can mend cracks that might otherwise grow into chasms. And by sincere, I mean genuinely acknowledging your mistake and how it affected your friend, not just throwing out a casual "sorry" and expecting it to do magic. There's no 'Ctrl+Z' in real life, but a heartfelt apology comes pretty close.

Even with the best navigational skills, some storms can't be weathered. If a friendship becomes toxic, continuously hurtful, or one-sided, it's okay to dock your ship and move on. There's a difference between weathering a storm and getting constantly shipwrecked. One makes you stronger; the other just leaves you feeling broken.

Remember, not all conflicts lead to the end of friendships. Some conflicts can actually make your bond stronger. They show you that your friendship can survive disagreements and misunderstandings. They teach you to communicate, understand each other better, and above all, they give you a glimpse into your own growth.

So next time you find yourself in the eye of a friendship storm, remember to breathe, communicate, and navigate with the understanding that the goal is resolution, not victory. Use your mistakes as lessons, your misunderstandings as opportunities for clarity, and your conflicts as a chance to strengthen your bond.

And remember, after every storm comes a rainbow. Or in our case, another episode of your favorite reality show, an extra sprinkling of that cheddar popcorn seasoning, and a bestie who's still by your side, ready to dive into the drama on screen rather than off it. Now, isn't that worth weathering a storm or two?

Chapter 3:

Love, Lust, and Everything In-Between

First Love and Heartbreak: The Rollercoaster of Emotions

First loves are a bit like jumping on a trampoline for the first time. It's exhilarating, a bit scary, and a real workout for your heart. There are those moments when you're soaring, suspended in the air, feeling like you're on top of the world. Then there are those moments where you land too hard or lose your balance and end up in a tangled, giggling heap. The highs are dazzling, the lows can be jarring, and through it all, you're experiencing something uniquely beautiful.

Remember the first time you saw them? The way your heart did a little tap dance in your chest, the way your stomach turned into a butterfly sanctuary, and your brain, your ever-dependable brain, decided to take a vacation. Suddenly, you found yourself tripping over air, laughing at their not-so-funny jokes, and trying to decipher the Da Vinci code that is their text messages.

Ah, the joy of first love! It's a heady mix of stolen glances, long conversations, shared secrets, and dreams intertwined. It's about discovering another person in a way you never have before and also discovering parts of yourself you never knew existed. It's about the thrill of the first kiss, the excitement of the first date, and the comfort of the first 'I love you.' It's about holding hands, and feeling like you've got the world at your fingertips.

But with the highs, come the lows. Because, you see, the thing about roller coasters is, what goes up, must come down. And sometimes, it comes down with a speed that takes your breath away. And that's where heartbreak enters the scene, not so much like a villain in a movie, but more like a bitter medicine that leaves a nasty aftertaste.

A broken heart feels a bit like a hangover, one minute you're in high spirits, and the next, you're nursing a pounding headache and a vague sense of regret. The world seems a bit too bright, a bit too loud. Your favorite songs turn into tear triggers, and your favorite places become memory mines.

But amidst the heartache and the tidal wave of emotions, there's a silver lining, a life-lesson gift-wrapped in tears and ice-cream tubs. Heartbreak teaches you resilience. It shows you that you can go through the emotional wringer and come out stronger on the other side.

It's like that trampoline again. Sometimes you fall, you lose your balance, you land too hard, and it hurts. But what do you do? You get back up. You dust yourself off. You take a deep breath, and you jump again. Because you know that the thrill of soaring, the joy of flying, the sense of liberation, it's all worth it.

First love and heartbreak, they're two sides of the same coin. Both can be intense, both can leave a mark, and both can change you in ways you never imagined. They're like the ultimate rollercoaster ride, full of twists and turns, peaks and valleys, screams and laughter. But at the end of the ride, you'll find that you've not only survived but also grown. You've learned, you've experienced, and you've lived.

So, here's to first love and heartbreak, to the beautiful rollercoaster of emotions they bring, and to you, brave rider, ready to take on the ride. After all, life is like a trampoline, and love, like jumping, is about having the courage to soar, the strength to fall, and the resilience to bounce back. So, buckle up, because it's going to be one hell of a ride!

Love vs Lust:
Deciphering Feelings

Picture this: you're in a dimly lit room, surrounded by people, and across the crowded space, your eyes land on them. Time slows down, your heart kicks up a notch, and you feel a warmth spreading through you. Ah, young love! Or is it lust? Perhaps a dash of both, sprinkled with a pinch of infatuation and a dollop of hormonal surges? Welcome to the sometimes confounding, often delightful, and universally human quest to decipher our feelings.

Love and lust, two tiny four-letter words, can stir up a whole pot of emotions, making us feel like we're walking through a maze blindfolded. But don't worry; this isn't a Greek tragedy, and you're not navigating the labyrinth alone. Let's put on our detective hats, grab our magnifying glasses, and unravel the mystery together.

Lust is like a sparkler on the Fourth of July. It burns bright and hot, capturing all your attention, but it fizzles out as quickly as it started. It's that physical attraction, the magnetic pull you feel towards someone. You know, the butterflies in your stomach, the rapid heartbeat, the 'I want to rip your clothes off' kind of passion. It's intense, it's exciting, and it's driven by desire.

But here's the catch. Just like how a sparkler, with all its dazzling light and heat, doesn't make a great long-term light source, lust doesn't often build a strong foundation for a deep, lasting relationship. That's not to say it's bad. Not at all! Lust can be fun, it can be thrilling, and it can teach you a lot about your desires and physical needs. But it's just one part of the equation.

Now, love, on the other hand, is like a carefully tended fire. It takes time to build, it requires patience, and it needs nurturing. Love goes beyond the physical. It's about genuinely caring for someone else, about wanting the best for them, about being there for them in both sunshine and storm.

While lust is focused on the present moment, the immediate gratification, love thinks in terms of a future. Love considers the other person's happiness as equal to your own. It's about understanding, respect, trust, and communication. Love makes you want to share your life, your dreams, your fears, and even your Netflix password.

That being said, things aren't always black and white. Sometimes, what starts as lust can grow into love. Other times, love might kick off with a spark of lust. They're not mutually exclusive, and they often mingle, creating a cocktail of emotions that's as intoxicating as it is complex.

Deciphering feelings isn't always easy. It's a bit like trying to solve a Rubik's Cube while riding a rollercoaster - dizzying, challenging, and a test of your patience. But remember, it's okay not to have all the answers. It's okay to explore, to experience, and to learn as you go. This is your journey, your story, and you get to write it one emotion, one experience, one relationship at a time.

So, whether you're feeling the rush of lust or the warmth of love, embrace it. Learn from it. Grow with it. Because in the end, whether we're talking about love, lust, or everything in-between, it's all part of this grand adventure we call life. And let's be real, it's this wild mix of emotions that adds the spice, the sweetness, and yes, sometimes the bitter taste to our life's journey. And without it, well, life would be as exciting as a salad without dressing. And who wants that?

The Art of Healthy Boundaries in Relationships

Think of your life as an exclusive party you're throwing. You've got great music, amazing food, a sparkling disco ball, and some fantastic guests. Now, imagine that you have no bouncer at the door of this party, and anyone can walk in and out as they please. The party that was supposed to be your joy-filled bubble suddenly becomes an open house for party crashers. Sounds like a nightmare, right? That's why you need boundaries in your life, just like you need a bouncer at your party. And this is doubly true when it comes to relationships.

Establishing healthy boundaries in a relationship is a bit like setting up the rules for a board game. It keeps things fair, prevents any 'cheating', and allows everyone to enjoy the game. But this isn't your typical Monopoly or Scrabble; this is the game of love, and trust me, it can get way more competitive and complex!

Boundaries define where you end, and where your partner begins. They're like invisible lines that protect your personal happiness, your integrity, and your identity. They are not walls to keep people out, but fences to ensure that both you and your partner can frolic freely without stepping on each other's toes.

Let's face it, sometimes, we romanticize the idea of two becoming one in a relationship. But here's a reality check - you're not a half waiting for another half to complete you. You're a whole on your own, and so is your partner. Boundaries ensure that while you're sharing a life together, you're not losing your individuality in the process.

There's a fine line between being considerate and losing yourself in a relationship. For instance, binging your partner's favorite reality show now and then is a sweet gesture. But if you're constantly suppressing your distaste for trash TV, and your daily routine starts revolving around 'Real Housewives' or 'Too Hot To Handle,' then Houston, we have a boundary problem!

Establishing boundaries can be as simple as saying 'No' to plans when you're tired, asking your partner to consult you before making decisions that affect you both, or standing your ground when they have a habit that bugs you. It's about letting them know what is acceptable to you and what is not, what makes you comfortable and what doesn't, what's your 'yes' and what's your 'no'.

But here's the tricky bit. Setting boundaries is not like a mic-drop moment. It's a conversation, a dialogue, a two-way street. It requires understanding, respect, and open communication from both sides. You're not a dictator laying down laws, but a partner seeking mutual happiness and fulfillment.

Also, just because you've set a boundary once doesn't mean it's set in stone. Our needs and comfort zones can change with time, and so can our boundaries. It's important to revisit them, discuss them, and adjust them if needed.

Now, I know what you're thinking. "This sounds great, but it also sounds like it might scare people away." And you know what, you're right. It might. But here's the thing - anyone who truly values you and your relationship will respect your boundaries. They're not obstacles or tests, but the foundation of a strong, healthy, and respectful relationship.

Remember, your boundaries are the bouncers at your life party. They help keep out the unnecessary drama, the disrespect, the energy vampires, and let in the understanding, the respect, the love. They help ensure that while you're having the time of your life, you're also comfortable, secure, and respected.

So, raise a toast to boundaries, my dear. May they always guard your heart, preserve your peace, and protect your sparkle in this wild dance of love. Because you, my friend, are the life of the party, and you deserve nothing less than a celebration that respects and honors you. Cheers!

Breaking Up Like A Pro

Oh, sweet thing! Have you ever tried to separate two pieces of super glued paper? It can get messy, right? Torn edges, residue glue, and quite possibly some swear words flying around the room. I get it, it's no fun. But you know what else can be a little like that? Breaking up. It can be messy, emotional, and sometimes even the cause of an emergency tub of ice cream (or two!). However, since breakups are a part of life as much as Netflix binges and prom nights, let's get you ready to handle them like a pro. Ready, steady, let's go!

1. Timing is Everything

First things first: do not–I repeat, do NOT–break up via text, email, or, heaven forbid, a post-it note (yes, I'm looking at you, Berger from Sex and the City). Your soon-to-be-ex deserves the courtesy of a face-to-face conversation. And timing is everything. Find a quiet and private place, ideally not at a time when they're already stressed or upset.

2. Get Your Ducks in a Row

Before you initiate the break-up, make sure you have a clear understanding of why you want to end the relationship. Are you unhappy? Do you want different things? Is the timing just off? Be honest with yourself first. This clarity will help make the conversation easier.

3. Keep It Real

Here's where you'll need a good dose of honesty and kindness. Make sure to express your feelings genuinely. Stick to 'I' statements like "I feel..." or "I need..." to communicate your emotions without blaming or criticizing the other person.

4. Don't Ghost!

What's scarier than a ghost? A ghoster! Simply disappearing out of someone's life without explanation is a big no-no. It's hurtful and unfair. If you feel the need to end a relationship, do it respectfully. Don't leave someone in the shadows.

5. Avoid the 'Let's Be Friends' Trap

Sure, it sounds like a nice idea, but in the fresh aftermath of a breakup, it's usually best to give each other some space. Jumping straight into a friendship might prevent you both from fully healing and moving on.

6. Handle the Aftermath

Post break-up, allow yourself some time to grieve. Yes, even if you were the one to end it. Breakups can feel like a loss, and it's important to acknowledge your feelings and let yourself heal. Surround yourself with your besties, keep busy, and do things that make you happy.

7. Remember: It's a Breakup, Not a Breakdown

Breakups can be tough, but remember, it's not the end of the world (even though it might feel like it). They're part of life and can help us grow, learn, and become stronger. As the saying goes, 'This too shall pass.'

8. Be Kind to Yourself

Finally, give yourself some love. Take a bubble bath, enjoy a Netflix binge, read a book, go for a run, eat some ice cream, do some yoga, or whatever else makes you feel good. You are important, and your feelings matter.

And that, darling, is how you break up like a pro. It might still be a bit messy, and yes, there might still be some metaphorical torn paper edges, but I promise you, it will get easier. You're stronger than you think, and remember, every ending is a new beginning in disguise.

"Is He Flirting With Me?"

Okay, okay, okay, I see that look in your eyes! You've been chatting with someone and there's a spark, a frisson, a sizzle... but hold on, is it just friendly banter, or is he actually flirting? Decoding the mysterious language of flirtation can sometimes feel like trying to understand an alien dialect, especially when your heart is fluttering faster than a hummingbird's wings. So, get your detective glasses on, queen, and let's start deciphering!

1. The Eyes are the Window...

...to flirtation! Seriously, watch those peepers. Is he making prolonged eye contact? That's usually a good sign. If he's looking deep into your eyes as if he's searching for a lost pirate's treasure, then there's a high chance he's flirting. And the eyebrow flash (a quick raise of the brows) when he first sees you? That's an almost universal sign of attraction!

2. The Smile that's More Than a Smile

Anyone can give a casual grin, but a genuine, lingering smile that reaches his eyes? That's what we're talking about! If his face lights up when he sees you, and he can't seem to stop smiling during your conversation, consider it a green flag.

3. Body Talks

Watch his body language. If he leans in when you're talking, mimics your gestures, or often touches his face, he's most likely into you. And if his feet and body are often pointed towards you, even when he's talking to someone else? Honey, that's not just the magnetic pull of your charm, that's a classic subconscious sign of attraction.

4. The Teasing Game

Remember when boys in the schoolyard would pull your pigtails and then run away? Well, sometimes, guys don't really outgrow that phase. They might tease you or playfully challenge you as a means of flirting. As long as it's all in good fun and not hurtful, enjoy the playful banter.

5. The Compliment Shower

If he's showering you with compliments like it's a confetti cannon at the end of a concert, that's a pretty solid hint. Especially if those compliments are specific and personal, like "You have an amazing laugh," or "You're really good at making people feel comfortable."

6. The Chatterbox Syndrome

People who are attracted to someone often can't help but want to talk to them. A lot. If he's engaging you in lengthy, in-depth conversations and seems genuinely interested in your opinions, there's a good chance he's flirting. And if he's sharing personal stories or discussing future plans with you? He's likely fishing for more than just friendship.

7. The Little Things Matter

Does he remember that you love mint chocolate chip ice cream or that you're allergic to cats? If he's paying attention to the little things about you, it shows he's invested in getting to know you more - a classic sign of flirting!

8. The Digital Flirt

In the age of social media and smartphones, digital flirting is a real thing! If he's always the first to like your posts, often comments, texts you, or floods you with memes that remind him of you, consider it a virtual wink.

But remember, these signs aren't foolproof. Everyone has their own unique flirting style, and sometimes, people are just naturally friendly. It's also important to trust your instincts - if it feels like flirting, it probably is!

Remember, girls, flirting should always be fun, respectful, and make you feel good about yourself. And if it turns out he is just being friendly? Hey, you've just gained a great buddy! So relax, have fun, and enjoy the sizzle of the flirt. Happy deciphering, lady!

Chapter 4:

The Crimson Wave: Making Peace with Your Period

From Embarrassment to Acceptance: Dealing with Period Stigma

If periods were a character in a high school drama, they would be that misunderstood bad boy that everyone talks about in hushed whispers. They show up uninvited, create chaos, leave you in discomfort, and yet, you can't imagine your life without them. Ah, periods, the unsung heroes of womanhood! And yet, the shroud of stigma around them is as persistent as those period cramps that just won't let you have a peaceful night's sleep.

Imagine you're on a covert mission every month. Your target - the restroom. Your equipment - a tampon or pad, cleverly hidden in your sleeve or bag. The objective - change your sanitary product without anyone knowing. Sound familiar? Oh, the lengths we go to hide something as natural as the changing of seasons or the waxing and waning of the moon!

So, let's start with the basics. Periods are not dirty, not shameful, not a 'womanly weakness.' They are a sign of a healthy body, a miracle of biology, a testament to the incredible strength and resilience that you possess. In short, periods are not a curse, but a superpower.

You bleed every month, endure discomfort and pain, go through mood swings that would put any rollercoaster to shame, and still carry on with your day-to-day life like a boss. If that's not superhuman, I don't know what is!

But how do we get past this period stigma? How do we transform this hushed whisper into a confident conversation? Here's where education and openness come in. The more we learn about our bodies, the more we normalize the conversation around periods, the closer we get to dismantling this age-old stigma.

Remember that covert mission we talked about earlier? It's time to abort it. Don't apologize for your period, don't hide it. If you need to change your tampon or pad, do so without the stealth of a secret agent. If you're in pain and need a hot water bottle, ask for it. If you're feeling emotional and need a bit of extra kindness, demand it.

Speak up about your experience, not just with your girlfriends, but with the boys too. Let's normalize men knowing about periods, understanding them, respecting them. After all, half the population has them for a significant part of their lives; it's high time the other half knew about them too!

Remember, shame thrives in silence, in secrecy, in the shadows. The moment you bring something into the light, talk about it, share it, the shame starts to lose its power. And that's what we need to do with periods. Bring them into the light, honor them, celebrate them.

So, the next time your period arrives, instead of whispering a quiet curse, why not throw a little period party? Buy yourself some fancy period products, binge on that chocolate, put on your coziest pajamas, and honor this incredible process your body goes through each month.

In the end, dealing with period stigma starts with accepting your period, embracing it, and proudly declaring to the world, "Yeah, I'm on my period. So what?" Because darling, your period is a part of you, and there's absolutely nothing about you that should be hidden, shamed, or stigmatized. You are a warrior, a goddess, a bleeding miracle. Own it!

Mastering Your Cycle: Tips and Tricks

Picture this: you're Indiana Jones and each month you embark on a daring adventure. Your trusty whip? Your knowledge of your own body. The ancient, booby-trapped temple? Your menstrual cycle. And like any skilled archeologist, it's time to dig deep and unlock the secrets of this treasure called 'Period.'

Getting to know your menstrual cycle is like learning a new dance. At first, the steps may seem awkward and confusing, but with time and practice, you'll find your rhythm and be salsa-ing your way through those 28-ish days like a pro.

First things first, get yourself a period tracking app. You wouldn't set sail without a map (unless you're feeling particularly pirate-y), so why navigate your menstrual cycle without one? There are plenty of great apps out there, and they'll help you predict your cycle, monitor your mood swings, and identify any unusual patterns.

Now let's talk about the main event - the period itself. Tampons, pads, menstrual cups, period panties - the world is your oyster when it comes to sanitary products. Try out different products to find out what suits you best. Remember, comfort is key, and what works for your BFF or your older sister might not work for you.

Now, onto the dreaded PMS. You know, that delightful time when you might turn into a werewolf or burst into tears because your sandwich is cut diagonally instead of straight. Don't fight these feelings, honor them. Think of it as your body's way of saying, "Hey, I'm about to do something incredible. I need a little extra care right now."

Create a PMS survival kit. Load up on your favorite snacks (chocolate has been known to work wonders), stock some comforting herbal teas, have a feel-good movie or book at the ready, and don't forget those pain relief options - be it a hot water bottle, some over-the-counter meds, or those yoga stretches that ease cramps.

Speaking of cramps, regular exercise throughout the month can help manage them. You don't have to transform into a CrossFit champion or a yoga guru; even a simple walk can work wonders. And when the cramps strike, gentle stretching or a warm bath can be surprisingly soothing.

Food plays a crucial role too. While you might crave greasy, sugary foods, your body needs nutrients to manage the menstrual marathon. Incorporate fruits, veggies, whole grains, lean proteins, and lots of water in your diet. But hey, if you want that slice of cake or that bag of chips, go for it! Periods are hard enough; you deserve a treat.

Sleep - your period's best friend and worst enemy. You need plenty of it, but it can be hard to get. Invest in some good-quality, comfortable sleepwear and beddings, keep your room dark and cool, and develop a pre-sleep routine to help you drift off more easily.

Last but not least, remember that while your period might feel like a monstrous wave crashing over you, it's your wave, your ride. Own it, master it, ride it out. You're not a damsel in distress, but a damsel dealing with her distress like a boss.

Your menstrual cycle isn't a secret code to be cracked, but a part of you to be understood, respected, and cared for. So, gear up, Indiana Jones, because the adventure awaits. And remember, no matter how treacherous the journey, you're the hero of this story. Now, whip that knowledge and master your cycle like the queen you are!

you

Your Body, Your Rules:
Feminine Hygiene Myths Debunked

The world of feminine hygiene is filled with more myths than a Greek mythology textbook, and it's about time someone played the Hercules and slayed those monsters. So, grab your sword, shield, and a comfy chair, because it's time to bust some period myths wide open.

Myth 1: You shouldn't bathe during your period. Who came up with this one, a smelly troll? If bathing wasn't important during your period, then why do you feel like a queen in a warm bath when cramps are trying to kick your butt? Bathe, shower, soak, bubble bath - whatever floats your boat, girl. Hygiene is crucial, period or not.

Myth 2: Tampons can break your hymen and steal your virginity. First, let's get one thing straight: a piece of tissue doesn't define your purity, worth, or virginity. Second, tampons are about as interested in your virginity as your laptop is in your love life. They're just there to do their job, not engage in scandalous behavior.

Myth 3: Using a menstrual cup is like performing a magic trick. Okay, so it might seem daunting at first, but so did learning to ride a bike or applying eyeliner, right? It's all about finding the right fold, the right angle, and then voila, you're a menstrual cup magician.

Myth 4: You shouldn't exercise during your period. On the contrary, dear reader, physical activity can help alleviate cramps and boost your mood. You don't have to run a marathon; even a gentle walk or some yoga can do the trick.

Myth 5: You're unclean or impure during your period. Let me roll my eyes so hard they reach another dimension. This isn't the Dark Ages, and you're not a witch to be dunked in a pond. You're a woman on her period, and that's as natural and clean as breathing.

Myth 6: Period blood is dirty. Nope, it's not dirty or toxic or evil. It's a mixture of blood and tissue lining your uterus. In fact, it's so clean you can use it to grow plants. Don't believe me? Look up 'menstrual blood plants.' Welcome to the future, where your period can literally give life to a dying plant!

Myth 7: You should hide your period like it's a state secret. Newsflash - it's not. So stop smuggling pads and tampons like they're illicit goods. Periods are not shameful, and there's no need to hide them.

Remember, girl, your body is not a riddle to be solved or a myth to be debunked. It's a glorious, miraculous masterpiece that you have the privilege of calling home. The next time someone tries to feed you a period myth, whip out your sword of knowledge and slay that beast.

Your body, your rules. Keep it clean, keep it healthy, keep it real, and keep being the fabulous period warrior that you are. Because, darling, you're not just surviving the crimson wave, you're surfing it like a pro!

Chapter 5:

Money Matters: Dollars and Sense

Earning, Saving, Spending, Budgeting: Managing Your First Paychecks

Welcome to the financial jungle, where money does indeed grow on trees. They're called jobs. And as you stand there, holding your shiny first paycheck, know this - you, my dear, are a lioness in this jungle. Money isn't just a piece of paper with a dead president's face on it; it's a tool, a resource, your ticket to the concert of independence. So, let's dive in, shall we?

Earning: When it comes to jobs, don't just leap at the first one that comes your way. Sure, it might seem tempting, especially when you're picturing that designer bag or dream vacation. But consider the job's suitability, your skillset, and if it aligns with your longer-term goals. Remember, you're not just a money-making machine; you're a powerhouse of potential waiting to be unleashed.

Saving: Consider each paycheck as a pizza. You wouldn't eat the whole thing in one go, would you? Well, okay, maybe you would. But with money, it's smarter to save a slice or two for later. Set up a savings account if you haven't already. Automate a small portion of your paycheck to go into this account. You'll thank yourself later when you've saved up enough for that big-ticket item or unexpected expense.

Spending: Ah, the siren song of spending. It's so easy to fall for its enchanting melody, especially with online shopping just a click away. But remember, just because you can buy something, doesn't mean you should. Try to differentiate between 'needs' and 'wants.' Your needs are the anchor keeping your ship steady in the stormy sea of spending. Your wants are more like seagulls; they may look cute and appealing, but they can quickly cause a mess if left unchecked.

Budgeting: Welcome to the least fun, but most essential part of managing money. Budgeting is like putting together a jigsaw puzzle. It might be frustrating at first, but once you get the hang of it, you'll see a clear picture of your financial health. Dedicate parts of your income to necessities, savings, and fun. Remember, all work and no play makes you a dull girl.

Investing: Imagine your money as little workers. Investing is about sending these workers out into the world to earn more money for you. It might seem scary at first, but with research and perhaps some guidance, you'll start to understand the basics. Think of investing as planting money trees that, with time and care, will bear fruit for future you to enjoy.

Remember, money is not the enemy, nor is it the goal. It's a tool that, when used wisely, can grant you independence, security, and opportunities. It's okay to make mistakes, to overspend one month or not save enough. As with everything else in life, managing money is a learning curve.

So, step into this jungle with confidence, lioness. Your journey to financial literacy has just begun, and though the path may seem treacherous at times, remember that you are smart, capable, and can conquer anything that comes your way. After all, you're not just making dollars and cents; you're making sense of your dollars. Now go on and roar, queen of the financial jungle!

Budgeting:
The Not-So-Fun but Oh-So-Crucial Game

Budgeting may sound as exciting as watching paint dry, but it's the secret ingredient in the recipe of financial success. Think of it like organizing your closet. You wouldn't toss everything in a pile, right? Unless you fancy diving into a clothing mountain every morning. The same goes for your money. It deserves its own organized space, so here's how to give it that:

Know your income: This is the money you earn from your job and any side hustles. Let's call this the 'wardrobe' of your financial closet. It's the space you have available to stash all your money clothes.

List your expenses: These are all the things you spend money on. Split them into fixed expenses (like rent, utilities, and insurance) and variable expenses (like eating out, entertainment, and shopping). Let's think of these as the 'clothes' you're trying to fit into your wardrobe.

Track your spending: This is where you play detective. For a month or so, track where every dollar goes. There are many apps to help with this, or you can go old school with a notebook. This step will show you what clothes you're wearing often, what's gathering dust, and what you forgot you even owned.

Set your budget: Now comes the arranging part. Based on your income and expenses, allocate money to different categories. A simple rule of thumb is the 50/30/20 rule: 50% of your income goes to needs (bills, groceries), 30% to wants (shopping, dining out), and 20% to savings. But feel free to tailor this to suit your unique style.

Adjust as necessary: Some months, you might need to buy a winter coat (unexpected expenses) or have money left over to buy a fancy dress (surplus). Be flexible with your budget and adjust as needed. Just make sure you're not squeezing your savings to make room for unnecessary spending.

Save for big-ticket items: Dreaming of a luxury handbag or a holiday? Rather than impulse buying and regretting later, plan and save for it. Break down the cost into smaller amounts and save over several months. It's like layaway, but with your own money and no interest.

Automate your savings: If you're the forgetful type or just like to make life easier, automate your savings. Set up an automatic transfer for a portion of your paycheck to go straight to your savings account. It's like having a personal assistant who ensures you're always wearing your savings shoes.

Review regularly: Just as you would clean out your closet regularly, review your budget, too. Maybe your income has changed, or your expenses have gone up or down. Keep your budget fresh and updated to reflect your current reality.

Remember, your budget is your financial roadmap. It helps you navigate from where you are now (broke college student) to where you want to be (financially independent boss babe). But don't stress too much if you stray off course occasionally. Budgeting is a skill that gets better with time and practice. Keep tweaking and adjusting until you find what works best for you. After all, your budget should be as unique and fabulous as you are. Happy budgeting!

Credit Cards, Loans, and Debts: The Financial Spice Rack

Welcome to the world of credit cards, loans, and debts! It's like entering the spice rack of your financial kitchen. Some spices, like your favorite cinnamon or paprika, enhance the flavor of your life. But, a heavy hand with the chili powder and woosh your tongue is on fire! Similarly, credit cards and loans can either spice up your life or set your finances ablaze.

So, let's explore this financial spice rack together, shall we?

Credit Cards: The Plastic Spice: Credit cards are like that vibrant turmeric powder. A little adds color to your life (Hello, online shopping! Hello, rewards!), but too much can leave a stain (Hello, massive bills! Hello, debt!). So, here's how to handle your credit card:

Budget First: Treat your credit card like a debit card. If you don't have the money in your account, don't spend it on your card. It's like adding spices while cooking. You can always add more, but you can't take it back once it's in there.

Pay on Time: Just as you wouldn't want your favorite TV show spoiled, you don't want to spoil your credit score with late payments. Set a reminder or automate payments to avoid late fees and interest.

Understand Your Statement: Get to know your credit card statement like your favorite rom-com. Look for any suspicious activity, understand how interest is calculated, and know your due dates.

Loans: The Necessary Nutmeg: At some point, you might need to borrow money for big-ticket items like education or a car. It's like adding nutmeg to a dish. It's essential, but too much can ruin your meal. Here's how to handle loans:

Understand the Terms: Know your interest rates, repayment schedule, and penalties for early or late payment. It's like reading a recipe before starting to cook.

Shop Around: Just as you would compare prices for that perfect dress, compare loan offers. A lower interest rate or better repayment terms can save you a lot of money.

Pay on Time: Just as in the world of Netflix, missing a due date has consequences. In this case, it can be a hefty fine or a ding on your credit score.

Debt: The Chili Powder of Finances: Nobody likes to be in debt. It's like accidentally adding too much chili powder to your food - it burns! But if you ever find yourself in debt, here's how to handle it:

Don't Ignore It: Debt doesn't disappear if you ignore it. It's like that pile of laundry you've been avoiding. It only gets bigger and scarier.

Make a Plan: Prioritize your debts. Start with the high-interest ones, or use the snowball method (clearing smaller debts first to gain momentum). Just like following a recipe, having a plan makes things manageable.

Seek Help: If your debt feels overwhelming, don't hesitate to get professional help. It's okay to ask for assistance when things get tough.

Remember, credit cards, loans, and debt aren't evil. They're simply tools in your financial toolbox. When used wisely, they can help build a stable and prosperous financial life.

So, put on your chef's hat, enter your financial kitchen, and start experimenting. And remember, just like in cooking, it's okay to make mistakes. That's how you learn and grow. Happy financing!

Investing for Your Future:
Money Grows on Trees...Sort Of

Well, you've figured out how to make money, how to budget it, how to use credit cards wisely, and how to tackle debt like a ninja. Now, let's talk about making your money work for you. Remember that silly phrase, "Money doesn't grow on trees"? Well, it's time to put on your imaginary green thumb because we're about to turn that on its head.

Investing is like having a magical bean that grows into a money tree. The money you earn is the bean, and the investment is the soil where you plant it. Over time, with a mix of sunlight, water, and a pinch of patience, it grows into a beautiful tree that starts to bear fruits, which in your case, are more money. Cool, right?

Now, before you get all excited and start dreaming about hammocks and Margaritas under your money tree, here's a reality check. Just like gardening, investing requires knowledge, care, and patience. But don't sweat, we've got you covered. Let's roll up our sleeves and get down to the nitty-gritty of investment gardening:

Investing is NOT Gambling: Repeat after me. Investing is NOT gambling. When you gamble, you leave everything up to chance. But when you invest, you make calculated decisions based on research and planning. It's like choosing what plants to grow in your garden based on your climate, soil type, and maintenance capacity.

Start Early, Start Small: There's a saying that the best time to plant a tree was 20 years ago, but the second best time is now. The same goes for investing. The earlier you start, the more time your money has to grow. Even if you only have a small amount to invest, go for it. Every big tree starts from a tiny seed, after all.

Diversify Your Portfolio: Translation: Don't plant just one type of tree in your garden. In the same way, don't put all your money in one type of investment. Mix it up. This way, if one plant doesn't do well, you'll have others that might thrive.

Ride Out the Storms: Just like your garden faces storms, droughts, and pests, the financial market also faces ups and downs. Don't panic when your investments take a hit. Keep calm, hold on, and trust that the storm will pass.

Regularly Review Your Investments: Just as you regularly check your garden for any signs of disease or pests, keep an eye on your investments. Monitor their performance, and don't hesitate to prune and tweak as needed.

Remember, investing isn't just about making more money. It's about planting the seeds for your future self. So, visualize what kind of garden you want to have in the future, and start planting those seeds today. And remember, the best gardener is not the one who has the most plants, but the one who takes care of them the best. Happy investing!

Chapter 6:

The Big "M": Considering Marriage

From Hollywood to Reality: Demystifying Marriage

Grab your popcorn, darling, it's time for a reality check! When it comes to marriage, we often get caught up in the Hollywood version of it, where every problem is resolved in 90 minutes, every kiss happens in the rain, and every couple lives happily ever after. But, *cue the dramatic music*, that's not how things play out in the real world.

Marriage isn't a rom-com; it's more like a never-ending season of a reality TV show, with a blend of The Great British Bake-Off, Survivor, and a dash of MythBusters. Intrigued? Let's dive in:

Marriage isn't Always a Piece of Cake: As much as we love those fluffy, frosting-covered baking shows, life isn't always sweet. There will be burnt cakes, collapsed souffles, and even baking disasters that set off the smoke alarm. But, it's all part of the experience. In a marriage, you'll have disagreements, differences, and even downright conflicts. But that doesn't mean your marriage is failing. It just means you're two distinct individuals trying to merge your lives. Like kneading dough, it takes effort, patience, and a bit of elbow grease.

Survivor, Marriage Edition: If you've ever seen an episode of Survivor, you know it's about teamwork, strategic planning, and resilience. Marriage is no different. You'll face challenges, make big decisions together, and sometimes, you'll need to survive on metaphorical coconuts and fish until the rescue boat (or payday) arrives. It's not just about survival, though. It's about thriving together, even when the going gets tough.

MythBusters: The Marriage Edition: "Married people don't argue," "You must have kids," "Marriage means the end of personal freedom," - Sound familiar? These are some common marriage myths that need some serious busting. Remember, every marriage is as unique as the people in it. There's no one-size-fits-all rulebook. You and your partner get to write your own rules, bust your own myths, and carve your own path.

Remember, marriage is a journey, not a destination. It's not always going to be a rosy, romantic, slow-motion run across a beach like in a Nicholas Sparks' movie. There will be moments of laughter, love, frustration, anger, joy, and everything in-between. But that's what makes it real, beautiful, and uniquely yours.

So, before you start daydreaming about that white dress or the perfect honeymoon, remember to take off your Hollywood-tinted glasses. Embrace the reality of marriage, with all its imperfections and surprises. After all, true love isn't about finding a perfect person. It's about seeing an imperfect person perfectly. Now, how's that for a plot twist?

When It's Right, It's Right: Timing and Marriage

Let's play a game. Imagine you're Goldilocks in the story of the three bears. You've just stumbled upon a charming cottage in the middle of a forest, and there are three plates of porridge on the table. One is too hot, the other too cold, and the third one...just right.

Think of timing in marriage as the porridge. Too early and it can burn you, too late and it might leave you cold. But when it's just right...ah, that's the sweet spot.

But, here's the catch. Unlike Goldilocks, who just needed to taste-test the porridge, figuring out the "just right" timing for marriage isn't as straightforward. It's a complex stew of personal readiness, emotional maturity, financial stability, and a dash of good old-fashioned gut instinct. And unlike a fairy tale, there's no one-size-fits-all narrative. So how do you figure out your "just right"?

Personal Readiness: Think of this as your basic recipe. This includes your individual growth, personal ambitions, and self-understanding. Are you ready to share your life with someone else? Have you lived the single life enough to appreciate the married one?

Emotional Maturity: This is the crucial ingredient in your marriage stew. Do you understand your emotions and can you handle them well? More importantly, can you understand and cope with someone else's emotions? Love isn't just about feeling butterflies in your stomach; it's also about navigating the storms together.

Financial Stability: Ah, the spicy bit! It's not about being rich, but about being responsible. Are you in a position to share financial responsibilities with someone else? Can you handle the added costs of a shared life?

Gut Instinct: This is the secret sauce. Sometimes, you just know. It's not about age or societal expectations, but about a deep, gut feeling. It's the inner voice that tells you that you're ready to commit to someone for life. Listen to it.

Remember, while society and Aunt Karen may have opinions on when you should get married, it's ultimately up to you. You're the chef of your life. Taste-test your decisions, adjust the ingredients, and cook it at your own pace. And when it's just right, you'll know. It'll be the perfect bowl of marriage stew, cooked to perfection, at the perfect temperature, ready for you to enjoy.

So, put on your chef's hat, take out your ladle of wisdom, and start preparing your recipe for the "just right" marriage timing. And remember, some of the best meals take time to cook. So, don't rush. Savor the process and trust that when it's right, you'll know. Bon appétit!

Single and Loving It:
You Don't Have to Say 'I Do'

Picture this: You're at a family gathering, everyone's having a good time, and then suddenly, a rogue aunt zeroes in on you, her eyes glinting with a single, all-consuming question, "So, when are you getting married?" The record scratches, the room goes silent, and all eyes are on you. If you've ever experienced this scenario, or can imagine it happening soon, this chapter's for you.

Let's set the record straight: marriage isn't a mandatory level in the game of life that everyone has to pass through. It's not a compulsory checkpoint or a boss level that you have to conquer to unlock the "happiness" achievement. It's a choice. And if you choose to remain single and love it, then hats off to you, girlfriend!

Here are some solid reasons why you might choose the single life:

Personal Growth: When you're single, you have a unique opportunity to focus on yourself without distractions. This is your time to explore, to discover what makes you tick, what makes your heart sing, and what makes you, you. Take this time to embrace self-love, to set personal goals, and to sprint towards them without carrying anyone else's baggage.

Freedom: Not to sound like a Disney princess yearning for more, but being single does mean freedom! You have the liberty to make decisions solely based on what's best for you. Want to move to another city? Do it. Want to eat ice cream for breakfast? No one's stopping you. The remote control of life is in your hands.

Financial Independence: When you're single, your money is your own. You get to decide how to spend or save every penny. Whether it's saving up for a dream vacation, investing in a startup, or buying that ridiculously overpriced but irresistibly cute pair of shoes - the financial decisions are yours alone.

Peace and Quiet: As amazing as relationships can be, they can also be noisy. And we're not talking about literal noise (though snoring can be a real problem, trust us). Being single can mean less drama, less compromise, and fewer arguments. It means having the bed all to yourself, and trust us, that's a luxury.

Waiting for the Right One: Maybe you've decided not to settle for anything less than butterflies. And that's okay. It's better to wait for the right one than to rush into a relationship just because you feel pressured.

Remember, choosing to be single doesn't mean you're "alone," "lonely," or "left on the shelf." It means you're strong enough to live and enjoy life on your own terms. It means you're brave enough to break the mold and dance to your own beat.

So, the next time someone asks you when you're getting married, just flash them a dazzling smile and say, "I'm single and loving it!" After all, your relationship status doesn't define you, you do. So, keep living your best single life, rockstar!

Chapter 7:

Voting:
The Power Is in Your Hands

The Importance of Your Vote:
Every Voice Matters

Picture this: it's karaoke night. You and your friends are excited, the atmosphere is electric, and everyone's name is in the hat for the next turn to sing. The DJ draws a name, and - surprise! - it's yours. You have the mic, you have the power to choose the next song. Would you give it away? No way, right? So why would you ever consider giving away your vote?

You might think that voting is like being a tiny drop in a vast ocean, that your one vote doesn't make a difference. But imagine if every drop in the ocean thought the same? There'd be no ocean left, only dry, parched land. Yikes!

Your vote is your voice, your power, your way of saying, "Hey, I live in this country and I have an opinion on how it should be run!" Here's why your vote matters:

Decision Making: When you vote, you're making choices about who will lead your local and national governments. These people make decisions on everything from the potholes in your street to national health care, environmental policies, and even how much you pay for university. So, if you want to have a say in these matters, you've got to vote.

Representation: Ever watched a movie where no one looked or sounded like you, or shared your experiences? Not very satisfying, is it? The same goes for politics. The more diverse the voters, the more diverse the leaders, and the more likely they'll be to understand and represent diverse perspectives.

Change: If you're unhappy with the status quo, or if you feel strongly about certain issues, voting is one way to effect change. It's like being in a group project - if you don't contribute, you can't complain about the results.

It's a Hard-Won Right: It wasn't long ago that women and minorities in the US were denied the right to vote. It took relentless struggle and resilience for us to earn this right, and each vote is a tribute to those who fought for us.

So, the next time you're feeling blasé about voting, remember the karaoke night. Would you give someone else the power to choose the song you're going to sing? No way! So why give them the power to decide how your country should be run? You've got the mic now, and every word you sing (or vote you cast) counts.

Remember, voting is not just a right, it's a responsibility. It's you, as a member of the band (or society), making sure your voice gets added to the mix. So, let your voice be heard, let your vote count. After all, you wouldn't let someone else choose your karaoke song, would you?

Navigating the Political Landscape: Parties, Policies, and More

So, you're ready to vote! Fantastic! But wait, what's this? A hundred candidates, a dozen parties, and a labyrinth of policies? Suddenly, voting feels a bit like trying to find your way around a new city without a map. So, let's build that map, shall we?

Think of political parties as your favorite brands. You have Nike, Adidas, Puma, and so on. Each has its own style, its own philosophy, its own vibe. Similarly, each political party has its own ideology, principles, and set of policies. The key is to find the one that fits you best.

Understand the Parties: In the US, the two main political parties are the Democrats (donkeys) and Republicans (elephants). But they're not the only game in town. You've got the Green Party, Libertarian Party, and others. Each party has its unique stance on issues like the economy, healthcare, education, and climate change. Do a little research, figure out where each party stands, and see which aligns with your values and priorities.

Meet the Candidates: You wouldn't go to prom with someone you haven't met, right? So, why vote for someone you don't know? Get to know your candidates - read about their beliefs, track records, and campaign promises. Check if their actions match their words. Do they walk the walk, or just talk the talk?

Decode the Policies: Policies can be as complicated as assembling IKEA furniture - loads of parts, tricky instructions, and what on earth is a 'Flärdfull'? But they're important. They're the blueprint of what a candidate or party plans to do if elected. So, take some time to understand them. Use trusted resources to break them down. Don't hesitate to ask questions and seek clarification.

Tune in to Debates: Debates are like the reality TV of politics. They're where candidates square off, defend their policies, and throw subtle (or not so subtle) shade at each other. Debates can give you a sense of a candidate's personality, thinking style, and ability to handle pressure. They're the political equivalent of an intense game of dodgeball.

Fact-Check: In the era of fake news and social media, it's easy to come across misleading information. Always verify the facts before forming an opinion. Remember, Google is your friend, but so are fact-checking websites. The truth is out there; you just have to dig a little.

Remember, you're not just voting for a candidate, you're voting for your future. So, make your decision count. Equip yourself with knowledge, be confident, and stride into that voting booth like it's the runway at New York Fashion Week. You're not just a voter; you're a decision-maker, a change-maker, a voice that matters. So, raise that voice, cast that vote, and make that difference. Your political landscape is yours to shape!

Voting Made Easy: Demystifying the Process

Alright, brace yourself because we're about to dive into the not-so-terrifying world of voting logistics. I know what you're thinking: "Isn't voting all about long lines, confusing forms, and old people in high-vis vests?" Well, you're not wrong, but it's also so much more. It's about you, your voice, and your power to shape your world.

Remember the first time you tried to order coffee at a fancy cafe? It was all "What the heck is a ristretto?" and "Is macchiato a type of pasta?" But then you figured it out, right? And now you strut in there like you own the place, sling your custom order like a pro, and sip your perfect brew with satisfaction. Voting is like that - confusing at first, but oh-so-empowering once you get the hang of it. So, let's get you to that power-sipping stage, shall we?

Register to Vote: This is the first step. It's like signing up for an online shopping site - you can't get the goods if you don't have an account. Check your state's registration deadline and criteria, fill out the form (either online or paper), and voila! You're a registered voter. You wouldn't believe how many people skip this step and then can't vote on election day. Don't be one of them!

Find Your Polling Place: Now, where do you go to vote? It's typically a nearby location like a school or community center. Don't worry; you're not expected to guess. You can find your designated polling place online. Think of it like the GPS that guides you to that hip new eatery everyone's talking about.

Know What's on the Ballot: Ballots are like menus - they list everything you have to choose from. But instead of tacos and burritos, you're choosing presidents, senators, and sometimes even policies. You can find a sample ballot online before election day. Study it, understand it, and know your choices.

Bring the Necessary ID: Some states require voters to show identification. Check what's required in your state and bring it along. It's like bringing your driver's license to a club - no ID, no entry.

Vote: This is it, the main event! You've researched, you've prepped, and now you're ready to cast your vote. So, you go to your polling place, get your ballot, fill it out (don't worry, instructions are provided), and submit it. Boom! You just voted. High five!

Consider Absentee or Early Voting: Can't make it on election day? No problem! Many states offer early voting or mail-in ballots. It's like Netflix for voting - watch (or vote) whenever, wherever.

Celebrate! You did it! You navigated the winding maze of voting and emerged victorious. Take a moment to appreciate yourself. Grab a cupcake, do a little dance, bask in the glory of your civic duty well done.

And there you have it - voting made easy! So, remember, voting isn't just a civic duty, it's a rite of passage. It's you stepping into your power, raising your voice, and saying, "Hey world, I'm here, I matter, and I'm not afraid to show it!"

Chapter 8:

Mental Health: It's Okay to Not Be Okay

The Silent Battle: Understanding Mental Health

Did you ever play The Floor is Lava as a kid? You'd leap from couch to coffee table, narrowly escaping certain "death," all the while giggling and screaming? Well, dealing with mental health is a bit like that, except instead of lava, you're trying to dodge a sea of invisible challenges. And instead of laughter and screams of joy, you might have tears and moments of silence. But here's the thing: just like The Floor is Lava, it's a game you can win.

You see, understanding mental health is kind of like realizing for the first time that your favorite reality TV show is scripted – it changes the way you see everything. Once you recognize that everyone is dealing with their own battles, the world looks a little different, and you might just start to feel a bit more understanding, and a lot less alone.

Let's start by breaking down the phrase "mental health." When we talk about physical health, it's easy to visualize – we picture running on a treadmill, eating veggies, or trying to touch our toes (and failing, most of the time). But when it comes to mental health, things get a bit blurrier, and that's because mental health is like the internet's invisible incognito mode – it's always there, but not always seen.

Mental health is a state of well-being, and it involves our emotional, psychological, and social self. It's how you feel about yourself, how you cope with the ups and downs of life, and how you relate to others. And just like your favorite band's most famous song, it affects everything.

Now, imagine for a second that your brain is a super complicated piece of software. It's got more tabs open than your browser during finals week, it's running background processes you didn't even know existed, and it's constantly getting updates (or in our case, life experiences) that can occasionally cause some glitches.

Mental health issues, such as depression, anxiety, and stress, are a lot like those glitches. They can be caused by a mix of genetic, biological, environmental, and psychological factors. Just like how you wouldn't blame your computer for getting a virus, it's important to know that mental health issues are not the fault of the individual experiencing them.

Having a mental health issue doesn't mean you're "crazy," "weak," or "broken." It just means your software needs a bit of troubleshooting. That might involve professional help like therapy or medication, or it might mean implementing lifestyle changes like more sleep, different nutrition, or mindfulness techniques.

It's important to know that it's perfectly okay to ask for help. In fact, it's brave. It's like being the first to hit the dance floor at a party – it takes guts, but it's totally worth it. There are countless resources and treatments available today, and they can genuinely help you to navigate your mental health.

So, you're probably wondering, "Okay, got it. But how do I know if

I'm just feeling down or if it's something more?" Great question. We'll dive into that later. But for now, remember: it's okay to not be okay. It's okay to ask for help. You're not alone in this invisible lava game. We're all in this together, leaping from couch to coffee table, navigating this thing called life.

Self-Care Isn't Selfish: Building Healthy Habits

Have you ever been on an airplane? If you have, you probably remember that part in the safety demo where they talk about the oxygen masks. The flight attendant always says, "Put your own mask on first before helping others." That's because you can't help anyone else if you're passed out from lack of oxygen, right? Well, that's a lot like self-care. And no, we're not talking about face masks and bubble baths (though those are pretty great too). We're talking about taking care of your mental well-being.

Self-care is like being your own superhero. You know, like in those movies where the hero finds out they have powers they never knew about, and they use them to kick butt and save the day? Except in this case, your superpower is making sure you're feeling the best you can be.

So, what does self-care look like? Well, it's like a choose-your-own-adventure book. It looks different for everyone. For you, it could be writing in a journal, going for a run, or screaming into your pillow (preferably when your roommates are out). For someone else, it might be a dance-off in the kitchen, a paint-by-numbers masterpiece, or a deep conversation with a friend.

Now, self-care isn't about being self-centered or narcissistic. It's about understanding what you need to do to take care of your mental health. It's not about ignoring the world and becoming a hermit. Although, spending a day alone, watching your favorite shows, and eating pizza does sound pretty good, right?

Building healthy habits is like building a fort when you were a kid. It takes some time and effort, and sometimes it might feel like it's about to fall over, but when it's done, it's your safe space. It's your go-to place when you need a break from everything.

When building your self-care habits, start small. Like, really small. Tiny. Minuscule. Think about it like you're learning a new dance routine. You don't start by jumping straight into the final choreography; you start with one step, then another, and another, until you're killing it on the dance floor.

Your self-care routine might start with taking ten minutes out of your day just to sit and breathe. It might be taking a short walk every day, or dedicating an hour every week to a hobby you love. Whatever it is, make it something that makes you feel good, something that helps you relax and recharge.

As you build these habits, remember that consistency is key. It's like learning to play an instrument – you can't just practice once and expect to be a pro. You need to stick with it, even when it feels hard, even when you don't feel like you're making progress.

Most importantly, remember that self-care isn't a one-and-done deal. It's a lifelong journey. There will be days when it feels easy, and there will be days when it feels like the hardest thing in the world. But just like learning to ride a bike or mastering the perfect winged eyeliner, once you've got it, it will become a part of you. And trust us, it's worth it.

And hey, remember that self-care also involves knowing when to reach out for help. Whether it's talking to a friend, a family member, or a professional, reaching out is a sign of strength, not weakness. So go on, put on your superhero cape, and start building your self-care fort. The world can wait while you take care of you. You've got this.

Just Feeling Blue or is it Something More? Understanding the Difference

If life was a giant color palette, emotions would be all the colors, with all their various hues and shades. You have your sunny yellows for joy, fiery reds for anger, and then there's the blue. The blues, my dear, are just as normal as the others. Everyone feels down sometimes, especially when dealing with stress, disappointments, or loss. But what happens when you feel like you've been caught in a never-ending rain cloud of gloom? When does "feeling blue" transition into something more significant? It's time to grab our emotional umbrellas and step into the rain.

1. Duration Matters

Everyone has off days, even off weeks. It's normal to feel down after a break-up, flunking a test, or watching the finale of your favorite TV show (I'm still not over some of them!). But if you find that your down-in-the-dumps mood is sticking around for more than two weeks, it might be more than just temporary blues.

2. It's Interfering With Your Life

When feeling down starts to interfere with your daily activities - school, work, social activities - that's a big red flag. If you're constantly canceling plans, falling behind in school, or calling out of work, you might be dealing with something more than just a case of the sads.

3. Changes in Appetite and Sleep

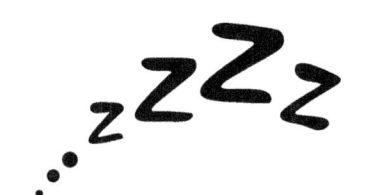

We all love a good midnight snack or a weekend sleep-in, but drastic changes in your appetite and sleep patterns can indicate something deeper. Eating significantly more or less? Sleeping all day or finding it hard to sleep at all? It could be a sign of a mental health concern.

4. Lack of Interest

Have you stopped enjoying things that you used to love? If your art supplies are collecting dust, your baking trays are staying in the cupboard, or your dance playlist remains unused, it may be cause for concern. A lack of interest in hobbies you once enjoyed can signal a mental health issue.

5. Unexplained Physical Symptoms

If you're feeling down and also have headaches, stomachaches, or just a constant sense of fatigue that can't be explained by physical causes, it could be a sign of a mental health concern. Remember, your mind and body are connected in more ways than one!

6. Emotional Numbness

Feeling blue is one thing, but feeling nothing at all? That's another. If you feel emotionally numb, disconnected, or just don't care about anything anymore, it might be time to reach out for help.

7. Thoughts of Self-Harm or Suicide

If you're feeling so low that you're having thoughts of self-harm or suicide, it's essential to reach out to a mental health professional immediately. Remember, there's no shame in asking for help, and there are resources available to support you.

So, feeling blue or something more? It can be tough to tell. After all, mental health isn't as clear-cut as a broken bone or a fever. But just like physical health, it's essential to take care of it. If you think you might be dealing with a mental health issue, please don't hesitate to seek help. Reach out to a trusted adult, a counselor, or a mental health hotline. Remember, asking for help isn't a sign of weakness, it's a sign of strength.

And even if it turns out you're just feeling blue, that's okay too. You're not alone, and it's okay to talk about it. After all, even the sky has cloudy days, but remember, the sun always comes out again. So let's put on our favorite music, cuddle up with a cozy blanket, and know that it's okay to not be okay.

Getting Help:
Therapy and Beyond

Let's start with a universal truth: asking for help does not make you weak. Actually, it's the complete opposite. It's like admitting you can't find your way in a new city without Google Maps. It doesn't mean you're incapable, it just means you're smart enough to use the resources available to navigate unfamiliar territory. So, let's start navigating the complex world of mental health support together, one hilarious yet insightful metaphor at a time.

Now, there's this old, dusty stereotype that therapy is just for the rich and famous, those with lots of time and money on their hands, right? Like, you probably imagine lying on a fancy leather couch in a room filled with mahogany bookshelves and a huge fireplace, while a person in a tweed blazer with elbow patches asks you about your childhood. But, babe, we're here to bust that myth.

First off, therapy is like a personal trainer, but for your mind. It's about getting stronger, more flexible, more resilient. It's about learning new skills and strategies to help you tackle life's challenges.

Choosing a therapist is a bit like dating. You might need to meet a few before you find the one that's right for you. Some people prefer a therapist who's like a wise owl, providing wisdom and insights. Others prefer a therapist who's more like a cheerleader, providing encouragement and support. And some prefer a therapist who's like a drill sergeant, providing tough love and hard truths. But unlike dating, it's perfectly okay to see more than one at a time. In fact, it's encouraged to try out a few to find the right fit!

You might also wonder about the price tag attached to therapy. Yes, it can be costly, but many therapists work on a sliding scale based on income. Plus, there are community mental health centers, online therapy options, and even school and university programs that offer affordable or free counseling. And girl, let me tell you, investing in your mental health is just as important as that cute new pair of shoes you've been eyeing. Well, probably more important, but who am I to judge?

There's also self-help and support groups, which are like group therapy with more snacks. These groups are led by trained professionals or peer leaders and can provide a sense of community and shared understanding. It's like a book club, but instead of discussing the plot twist in the latest bestseller, you discuss life's plot twists.

Now, therapy is not always about talking. There's also art therapy, music therapy, and dance therapy, to name a few. These therapies can be an amazing way to express what you're feeling without having to find the words. It's like creating your own personal soundtrack or art gallery that reflects your inner world.

Of course, mental health support can also include medication. And no, taking medication for your mental health is not a sign of weakness, just like wearing glasses isn't a sign of weakness. Both are tools to help you see the world more clearly.

Navigating mental health can be tricky. It's like learning to ride a bike without training wheels for the first time. You might wobble, you might fall, but with the right support, you'll be cruising down the road in no time. Remember, it's okay to ask for directions. In fact, it's more than okay, it's brave. And we all know you've got bravery in spades, right?

Chapter 9:

College or Not: Making the Big Decision

University 101:
The Pros and Cons

Ah, the question that looms over every fresh 18-year-old: to university or not to university? It's a question that can bring you a headache faster than a poorly mixed party punch. But fear not, dear reader, let's discuss this over a metaphorical cup of calming chamomile tea.

So, let's start with the shiny stuff, the glitters and gold of university life: the pros.

Pro #1: Knowledge. I'm not talking about just any kind of knowledge like "how many types of cheese exist?" (over 2000, by the way). I'm talking about deep, thought-provoking, universe-expanding knowledge in a subject you're passionate about. It's like your brain goes to the gym and comes out with a six-pack of intellect.

Pro #2: Skills. Aside from learning how to survive on ramen noodles and instant coffee, you will acquire some serious skills in your chosen field. You'll be prepared for a range of careers and, on top of that, you'll also learn how to problem solve, communicate, and collaborate. These are the kind of skills employers are hungrier for than a vegan at a salad bar.

Pro #3: Connections. University is like the ultimate networking event, minus the boring small talk and business cards. You get to meet people from different backgrounds, cultures, and perspectives. These could be your future colleagues, collaborators, or even your future business partners.

Now that we've dipped our toes into the rainbow-coloured waters of university life, let's wade into the murkier bits: the cons.

Con #1: Cost. University is like a designer handbag: sleek, coveted, but yikes, it comes with a hefty price tag. Tuition, textbooks, and housing can add up to a significant sum. It's the kind of bill that can make your wallet feel lighter than a feather in a windstorm.

Con #2: Time. A university degree usually takes at least four years to complete. That's a big chunk of your youth. It's the equivalent of 1,460 days, or 35,040 hours, or 2,102,400 minutes! But hey, who's counting?

Con #3: No guarantee. Despite what we'd love to believe, a university degree doesn't come with a 100% job guarantee. It's a bit like buying a lottery ticket – it might improve your odds, but it doesn't assure you a win.

Whether or not to go to university is a big decision, kind of like deciding whether or not to chop off your long hair. It's personal, it's consequential, and it's a choice only you can make. Just remember, whether you opt for a pixie cut or flowing locks, the important thing is that it's the right choice for you. Similarly, whether you opt for university or a different path, the important thing is that it's the right choice for your future.

Exploring Alternatives:
Trade Schools, Gap Years, and More

Let's say, hypothetically, you've decided that the university route, with its lecture halls and quirky professors, isn't your cup of tea. Maybe you're eyeing that cup of tea suspiciously, wondering if it's spiked with overwhelming debt and existential dread. And that's okay! There are as many paths to success as there are Ben & Jerry's flavors. Let's talk about a few.

First off: trade schools. If university is a sprawling buffet, trade schools are like specialty food trucks: focused, high-quality, and way less time-consuming. You want to be a pastry chef? There's a school for that. Electrician? School for that. Massage therapist, interior designer, or paralegal? Yep, schools for those, too. The great thing about trade schools is that they give you practical, hands-on training in a specific field, often in less time than a traditional university degree.

Next, let's discuss gap years. Some people hear 'gap year' and imagine a year-long vacation filled with beach lounging and late-night parties. If that's your vibe, cool! But a gap year can be so much more. It could be a year spent volunteering, interning, or working to save money. Maybe it's a year spent traveling, learning new languages and cultures. Or perhaps it's a year spent exploring passions and hobbies that you didn't have time to pursue before. A gap year isn't a pause on life; it's just a different song.

Apprenticeships are another fantastic option. They're like the 'learn-on-the-job' version of trade school. You get paired with a skilled professional in your desired field and learn by doing, all while getting paid. It's like getting a free backstage pass to a concert, where the concert is your future career.

There's also the self-taught route. Say you have a passion for graphic design, coding, or creative writing. There are countless resources online – blogs, tutorials, online courses – where you can learn at your own pace. Who knows? Your bedroom could be the birthplace of the next big mobile app or bestselling novel.

Lastly, let's not forget entrepreneurship. If you've got a killer business idea and the passion to match, why wait? Some of the world's most successful entrepreneurs started their businesses fresh out of high school (or even before). Starting a business can be like riding a rollercoaster blindfolded, but if you're up for the thrill, it can lead to incredible heights.

Remember, life isn't a race; it's a choose-your-own-adventure novel. Some paths might be longer, some might be winding, and some might lead you back to where you started. But that's okay! As long as you keep turning the pages, you're heading in the right direction.

Surviving the Pressure: Choosing What's Best for You

As you teeter on the edge of adulthood, you may feel like you're participating in an episode of "American Ninja Warrior," dodging expectations and judgments instead of giant spinning blades. Family members may ask, "What do you plan to do after high school?" Friends might say, "I got into three colleges, what about you?" And amidst all this, your heart is screaming, "I just want to live my life!"

When it comes to making big decisions about your future, it's easy to feel like you're being buried under a mountain of unsolicited advice and expectations. It's like being the target in a dodgeball game where everyone's throwing their opinions, and you're desperately trying to dodge or catch, all while avoiding a face-plant.

But remember, you're the hero of your own story, not a side character in someone else's. So, what does the hero do? They dig deep, find their courage, and decide what's best for them, not for Aunt Karen or Cousin Joe.

First and foremost, it's essential to listen–to really listen–to your inner voice. Sometimes, that voice gets drowned out in the cacophony of expectations. To hear it clearly, you might need some silence. Do what you need to find that silence. Go for a long walk, meditate, write in a journal–whatever helps you tune out the world and tune into yourself.

Next, do your research. Ignorance isn't bliss when it comes to planning your future. Look into the realities of each path. Talk to people who've walked them. Shadow a professional, take a tour of a trade school, spend a day at a university, or speak with an entrepreneur. Arm yourself with knowledge so you can make an informed decision.

Also, don't shy away from seeking professional guidance. Career counselors, academic advisors, and guidance counselors are there for a reason. They're like personal trainers for your future, helping you figure out your strengths, weaknesses, and how to reach your goals.

Try to avoid the comparison trap. Your journey isn't a multi-player game; it's a solo adventure. Your best friend might be gearing up for med school while you're preparing for a gap year backpacking through Europe. Your paths are different, and that's okay! As Dr. Seuss wisely said, "Today you are You, that is truer than true. There is no one alive who is Youer than You."

Finally, allow yourself the freedom to change your mind. If you start down a path and realize it's not for you, it's okay to turn around or take a detour. Remember, you're not a GPS system pre-programmed to a specific destination; you're an explorer charting your unique course.

Life isn't about having a perfect plan; it's about being true to yourself. When you feel the weight of the world on your shoulders, take a deep breath, square your shoulders, and remind yourself, "I got this." Because you really, really do.

Chapter 10:

Body Image: Embracing the Skin You're In

The Mirror Lies:
Confronting Body Dysmorphia

If your mirror could talk, what would it say? Would it shower you with the compliments you deserve or morph into a snarky critic, picking at every imperfection? Unfortunately, for many of us, our mirrors seem to have developed the personality of a sour-faced, nasty-tongued stepmother from a Grimm's fairytale. But remember, mirrors only reflect what we want to see, not what is the absolute reality.

Body dysmorphia is like having an Instagram filter permanently stuck on selfie mode, and not one of the cute ones that gives you puppy ears. It's one that distorts your image, blows your flaws out of proportion, and makes you feel like the Ugly Duckling who never turned into a swan.

But let's get real, and not "reality TV" real, but really real. Everyone, and I mean everyone, has things about their body they don't like. Maybe it's a freckle shaped like Nebraska, a cowlick that refuses to be tamed, or love handles that are a little too fond of hanging on. But that's just part of being human. Our bodies are unique, they tell our stories, and those so-called imperfections? They're the punctuation marks in our narrative.

Learning to confront body dysmorphia begins with acknowledging that your perception is skewed, like looking through a funhouse mirror. Those extra-long legs aren't real, and neither is the warped perception you have of your own body.

Next, consider seeking professional help. Therapists and counselors are like personal trainers for your mind, helping you flex your mental muscles and conquer negative thoughts. They can provide you with strategies and tools to combat body dysmorphia, helping you to see your true reflection, not the distorted image your mind may be conjuring up.

Try practicing mindfulness. Mindfulness isn't some New Age fluff—it's a powerful tool for staying present and grounded. So, rather than focusing on how your body looks, pay attention to what it can do. Can it dance like no one's watching? Can it hold a yoga pose like a boss? Can it snuggle a puppy, paint a picture, or whip up a mean batch of cookies? That's pretty darn amazing if you ask me.

It's also important to clean up your social media diet. If your feed is filled with photoshopped models and unrealistic beauty standards, it's time for a purge. Unfollow accounts that make you feel less than and replace them with ones that uplift and inspire you.

Remind yourself daily that your worth isn't defined by your waist size, the gap between your thighs, or the clearness of your skin. Your worth is inherent, infinite, and unchangeable. And most importantly, you are more than a reflection in a mirror.

Facing body dysmorphia is like walking through a dark tunnel. It can be scary and you might feel lost at times, but remember, there's light at the end. So keep walking, keep fighting, and keep believing in the beautiful person you are. Because you're not just a reflection—you're a whole universe of wonder.

Health vs Size: Understanding the Difference

Whoever decided that health and size are synonymous deserves to be trapped in a room filled with IKEA furniture and no instruction manual. You know, the kind of confusing, complex pieces that always end with a leftover screw, a few too many swear words, and a lingering fear that your newly assembled wardrobe might collapse at any moment.

But I digress. Here's the truth: health and size are not two peas in a pod. They're more like distant cousins—twice removed. To put it in social media terms, if health and size were on Facebook, their relationship status would be "it's complicated".

Firstly, let's debunk the myth that being thin automatically equates to being healthy. Skinny bodies can be just as unhealthy as larger ones. Ever heard of Skinny Fat? Nope, it's not the latest hipster band or vegan alternative to pork rinds. It's a term for individuals who look slim but have high amounts of body fat and low muscle mass, often due to poor diet and lack of exercise.

On the flip side, individuals with larger bodies can be healthy, too. The size of your jeans doesn't determine how far you can run, how strong you are, or how much endurance you have. There are plus-sized athletes out there crushing marathons, weight lifting records, and the stigma that size defines athletic ability.

But let's get back to you. You, darling, are not a size, a number on a scale, or a mannequin in a store window. You are a complex, beautiful, living, breathing human being. And what matters most isn't the size of your body, but the state of your health.

To truly understand the difference between health and size, you need to redefine your understanding of health. Health is not a one-size-fits-all term. It's a multifaceted blend of physical, mental, and emotional wellbeing. Health is eating nutritious foods, but also treating yourself to ice cream on a hot day. It's jogging in the park, but also enjoying a Netflix marathon on the couch. It's expressing your feelings, seeking support when needed, and taking time for self-care.

Now, this doesn't mean you should totally ignore the number on the scale or the size of your clothes. But rather than obsessing over these numbers, use them as one of many tools to assess your health. Regular check-ups with your doctor, blood tests, how well you sleep, your energy levels, your mood—these are all equally important indicators of your health.

Lastly, remember that your health is a journey, not a destination. There will be twists, turns, bumps, and detours. There will be days when you eat your veggies, and days when you eat the entire pizza. That's okay. That's life. The key is balance and listening to your body.

So, ditch the idea that size equals health. Because in the end, it's not about the size of the boat, but the motion of the ocean, right?

Be healthy, be happy, be you—no matter what size or shape that comes in.

Celebrating You:
Tips for Positive Body Image

Well hello there, beautiful! Wait, did you just roll your eyes or make a sarcastic comment under your breath? If so, hit the pause button. Let's tackle that reaction. Because, in case you forgot, you are drop-dead, no-doubt-about-it, stop-traffic-on-a-busy-street gorgeous. And I'm not just talking about your external appearance. You, my dear, are beautiful inside and out.

But here's the thing. It's so easy to forget this simple truth when we're bombarded with photoshopped images, "perfect" Instagram influencers, and the societal pressure to look a certain way. It's like trying to enjoy a picnic in a hurricane. It's just not fair.

So, how can you keep your picnic blanket firmly on the ground and enjoy the feast of life without worrying about unrealistic beauty standards? The answer is nurturing positive body image. But how do we get there? Buckle up, sunshine, and let's dive into some tips.

1. Meet Your Best Friend: The Mirror

Make a date with your mirror every day, and no, it's not to nitpick at your flaws. Stand in front of the mirror and find three things you love about yourself. Maybe it's your freckles, the way your eyes sparkle when you laugh, or your strong thighs that can kick a soccer ball halfway across the field. Appreciate your body for all the incredible things it allows you to do. It's more than just an object—it's your vehicle through life.

2. Don't Believe Everything You See

Whether it's magazines, Instagram, or movies, remember that what you're seeing is often not reality. Photos are photoshopped, lighting is manipulated, and even the "perfect" people feel insecure. So next time you find yourself comparing your body to someone else's, hit the mental brakes and remember that comparison is the thief of joy.

3. Keep Your Thoughts Positive

Every time a negative thought about your body pops up, visualize a big, red stop sign. Then, replace it with a positive thought. It might feel silly at first, but with practice, positive thoughts will become your default.

4. Surround Yourself with Positivity

If you have friends who constantly diet, criticize their bodies, or make you feel bad about yours, it's time to expand your social circle. Seek out people who love and respect their bodies and encourage you to do the same. Positivity is contagious—catch it!

5. Practice Self-Care

Taking care of your body goes a long way in fostering a positive body image. This means eating nutritious food, exercising regularly, getting enough sleep, and taking time for relaxation and fun. Remember, self-care isn't just about your body—it's about your mind and soul, too.

6. Wear What Makes You Feel Good

Forget fashion "rules" and wear what you love. If you feel great in a polka dot onesie, rock it! If high heels make you feel like a goddess, strut your stuff. Your style should be a reflection of you, not what some fashion magazine dictates.

7. Seek Support When Needed

If your body image is causing you distress or leading to unhealthy behaviors, seek help. Therapists, counselors, and support groups can provide valuable tools to help you navigate your feelings and build a positive body image.

Remember, having a positive body image doesn't mean you think your body is perfect. It means you appreciate, respect, and accept your body as it is, celebrating all the incredible things it can do. It's a journey, not a destination, and there's no time like the present to start your adventure. So go on, embrace and celebrate the skin you're in—you're worth it!

Building a Supportive Community: Surrounding Yourself with Positive Influences

Let's take a moment and think about your favorite comfort food. The one that warms you up from the inside, that you crave on a rainy day or after a long week. Now, picture being in a room filled with people who are that comforting, warm, and satisfying. Pretty awesome, right? That's what it feels like to be surrounded by a supportive community. No, I'm not suggesting you eat your friends (please don't), but your chosen tribe should be as good for your soul as your go-to comfort food is for your taste buds.

But here's the catch, in this Instagram-perfect world, finding the right group can feel like navigating a minefield. It's so easy to stumble into toxic or negative influences that can affect your body image. Here's your guide to creating a supportive, body-positive community that will not only have your back but also cheer you on.

1. Recognize the Good

Just like how every rom-com starts with the leads unaware they're perfect for each other, you might not realize you're already surrounded by some positive influences. It could be your best friend who always uplifts you, your sibling who celebrates your wins, no matter how small, or your favorite teacher who sees your potential. Acknowledge these cheerleaders in your life and try to spend more time with them.

2. Clean Up Your Social Media Feed

Let's face it, we spend a lot of time scrolling through our feeds. If your Instagram looks like an unattainable highlight reel of picture-perfect bodies, it's time for a detox. Unfollow accounts that make you feel less about yourself and follow ones that promote body positivity. Go for diversity, authenticity, and accounts that spark joy. Your feed should feel like a friendly brunch, not a beauty pageant.

3. Clubs, Groups, and Organizations

Whether online or in real life, joining groups that share your interests can be a great way to find your tribe. Into books? Join a book club. Love to run? How about a local running group? Fan of knitting? There's a club for that, too! Shared interests can be a great foundation for supportive relationships.

4. Learn to Disengage

Not every negative influence needs confrontation. Sometimes, the best thing you can do is step back. If someone constantly criticizes your appearance or compares you to others, it's okay to distance yourself. You're not a dumping ground for someone else's insecurities.

5. Be the Positive Influence

"Be the change you wish to see in the world" - yeah, Gandhi

definitely knew what he was talking about. Try to be the positive influence in someone else's life. Compliment your friends on things that aren't appearance-based. Celebrate their intelligence, their kindness, their strength. After all, what goes around comes around.

Building a supportive community isn't an overnight task, but it's an investment worth making. A good tribe can not only help you embrace the skin you're in but also help you grow into the best version of yourself. And remember, girl, you're a limited edition. So find a group that celebrates that, and you'll be one step closer to loving yourself, every day, no filter needed. Now, doesn't that sound tastier than any comfort food?

Self-Care and Body Positivity: Practicing Love and Acceptance

You know when you're scrolling through Netflix, trying to find something to watch, and you see a movie you've already seen like a thousand times, but you click on it anyway because it feels like a warm blanket? Well, practicing self-care is like clicking on that movie. It's like gifting yourself a big hug. And body positivity? That's like the popcorn that makes the movie even better.

Let's break this down:

1. Self-Care: The Movie That Never Gets Old

Self-care isn't just about face masks and bubble baths, though those are awesome and totally count! It's about dedicating time to care for your mind, body, and soul. It's about understanding what YOU need and acting on it. Let's look at some examples:

Physical self-care: This includes everything from dancing like a maniac to your favorite Taylor Swift song to getting eight hours of sleep. Eat nutritious food that fuels your body and makes you feel good. It's like saying to your body, "Hey, I've got you."

Mental self-care: Remember when you were a kid, and you used to lose yourself in a good book or draw just because? Well, it's time to channel your inner child and do something that stimulates your mind. Read, write, draw, solve puzzles, anything that makes your mind happy.

Emotional self-care: Ever wish you could turn off your emotions? Yeah, we've all been there. But instead of wishing them away, let's acknowledge them. Journal your thoughts, meditate, or just cry it out while watching 'The Notebook' for the hundredth time. Let yourself feel without judgment.

Social self-care: This is about surrounding yourself with people who light you up. It could be calling your best friend for a chat, having a family game night, or attending a Zoom party. Remember, humans are social animals; even the introverts among us need some level of social interaction.

2. Body Positivity: The Delicious Popcorn

While self-care is about your holistic well-being, body positivity is specifically about loving and accepting your physical self. It's about looking in the mirror and saying, "I am enough, just as I am." Here are some tips to boost your body positivity:

Change the narrative: Instead of focusing on what you don't like about your body, focus on what it allows you to do. Those legs? They allow you to walk, run, and dance. Your hands? They let you create, touch, and feel. Your body is an incredible instrument; appreciate it!

Dress for confidence: Wear clothes that make you feel good, not because they're trendy or someone else likes them. Your style, your rules.

Stop comparing: Your body is unique to you. Comparing it to others is like comparing a cat to a dog. They're different, and they're both beautiful.

Practice gratitude: Every night before bed, think of three things you love about your body. It could be as simple as "I love how my eyes crinkle when I laugh" or "I love that my body carried me through the day."

Remember, self-care and body positivity aren't destinations; they're journeys. Some days will be harder than others, and that's okay. The important thing is to keep moving forward, one step at a time. So, queue up your favorite self-care activities, grab a bowl of body positivity, and get ready to enjoy the beautiful movie of your life, starring the one and only fabulous you!

Chapter 11:

The Highlight Reel: Understanding the Illusion

The Highlight Reel: Understanding the Illusion

Picture this: You're scrolling through Instagram, sipping on your pumpkin spice latte, when you see it. A picture of your classmate, Mary, posing on a beach in a bikini, looking like she stepped out of a fashion magazine. Instantly, you feel a knot in your stomach. Why don't you look like that? Why aren't you on a beach? Heck, why isn't your life as perfect as Mary's appears to be?

Hold up, and rewind for a second. That right there? That's the social media illusion, my dear friend. It's like seeing a magician saw someone in half. It looks real, but it isn't. Welcome to the world of the Highlight Reel.

Social media is like a glossy magazine; it showcases the best of the best. It's the glitz, the glam, the amazing holidays, and perfect bodies. It's a world where acne doesn't exist, hair is always shiny, and everybody seems to be living their best life 24/7. But here's the spoiler alert: it's not reality.

Behind The Curtain

Think about it. How often do you post pictures of yourself when you're feeling low, haven't washed your hair in three days, or when you're in your pajamas eating cereal straight from the box? Probably not a lot, right? Now, what if I told you Mary is the same? Sure, she looks fabulous on that beach, but what you don't see is the 50 other photos she didn't post because she thought her nose looked too big, or her stomach wasn't flat enough.

The Comparison Trap

When we scroll through social media and compare ourselves to what we see, we're comparing our 'behind the scenes' with someone else's 'highlight reel.' It's like comparing a raw, unedited film to a blockbuster movie. One is real and raw; the other is edited, polished, and carefully curated. Comparing these two would be unfair, wouldn't it?

Your Reality, Your Rules

Remember, you have the power to choose what you consume on social media. If an account makes you feel bad about yourself, hit the unfollow button. It's like cleaning your room; get rid of what no longer serves you.

Embrace the Unfiltered

But what if we all started sharing a bit more of the unfiltered, unedited moments? What if, for every posed photo, we shared a candid, too? What if, for every success story, we shared a failure, too? We could make social media a bit more real, a bit more honest, and a lot less stressful.

So next time you find yourself spiraling into the comparison trap, remember that you're only seeing a snippet of someone's life. Their highlight reel. You don't see their struggles, their fears, their insecurities.

Remember, it's okay not to have a perfect life, because honestly, nobody does. Not even Mary. Instead of comparing yourself to others, focus on your journey, your growth, and the person you're becoming. Because, darling, the real you is more than enough, and that's no illusion. Now, go ahead and double-tap that thought!

Social Media Detox: Taking Time Off

Okay, time to spill some tea. You know how your phone shows you the screen time reports every week? Ever looked at it and thought, "Wait, how did I spend THAT many hours on Instagram?" Well, welcome to the club, girl! We've all been there, wondering how the minutes turned into hours while we mindlessly scrolled through social media.

Imagine all the things we could do if we got that time back! We could learn to play the ukulele, bake the perfect sourdough bread, or even binge-watch an entire season of that new Netflix show (okay, maybe that's not so different, but at least it's an intentional choice, right?).

Jokes aside, have you ever thought about doing a social media detox? Yes, like a juice cleanse, but for your digital life. It's about breaking free from the chains of our digital devices and experiencing life in high definition - the real world.

But Why Detox?

Good question, my friend! So, we already established that social media can gobble up our time like a hungry Pac-Man. But it's more than that. Ever felt drained, anxious, or even a tad depressed after a social media binge? That's called digital fatigue, and it's real. A detox could help refresh your mind, restore your focus, and renew your perspective. Sounds pretty chill, right?

Ready, Set, Detox!

So how do you do a social media detox? It's simple - take a break from social media. It could be for a day, a week, or even a month, whatever works for you. The idea is to disconnect to reconnect with yourself and the world around you.

But, and there's always a 'but', be prepared. It's not going to be a walk in the park. At first, your fingers might itch to open that Instagram app or tweet your thoughts on the latest episode of your favorite show. That's okay. You're rewiring your habits, and it's going to take some time.

Be Productive, Not Just Busy

During your detox, find things to do that you love or want to try. This isn't about swapping screen time for couch time (though there's nothing wrong with a little R&R!). Get active, be creative, explore nature, write in your journal, catch up with friends in person, read that book you've been meaning to read. Remember, the goal is to live more in the moment.

Re-entry: Coming Back with a Plan

When you're ready to return to the digital world, have a plan. Maybe set boundaries, like no social media after dinner, or maybe you only check your apps twice a day. The idea is to have control over your social media usage, not the other way around.

Doing a social media detox is like doing spring cleaning for your mind. It might seem challenging at first, but once you've done it, you'll feel lighter, brighter, and ready to take on the world. And the best part? You can do it anytime you feel the need to hit the reset button on your digital life.

So, are you ready to swap the blue light of your screen for the blue sky of a tech-free day? It's time for a social media detox. And who knows, you might just find that the world outside your screen is just as, if not more, Instagram-worthy!

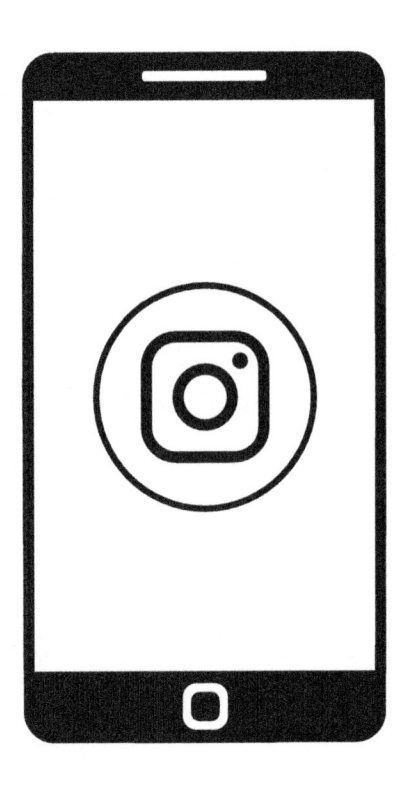

Creating a Positive Online Presence

Alright, imagine this: you're on a first date, and your date leans over, pulls out his phone, and Googles you right there on the spot. Don't act so shocked; we live in the digital age after all! What would he find? A string of party pics, a well-crafted inspirational quote on a sunset background, or maybe, just maybe, a video of you dancing in your PJs to the latest TikTok challenge? Yikes!

So, the million-dollar question: how can you create a positive online presence? Well, worry not, because your girl has got you covered!

#1 Be Authentic

First things first, stay true to yourself. Show the real, unfiltered you. We're talking about your interests, passions, and what makes you, well, YOU. If you love books, share your latest reads. If you're into cooking, post that fabulous brunch you made. Your profile should be a reflection of who you are and not a carbon copy of someone else's. Remember, every time you post, you're adding to your digital self-portrait.

#2 Mind Your Manners

Just because you're behind a screen doesn't mean you can forget your manners. The golden rule applies in the digital world, too: treat others how you want to be treated. Be kind, respectful, and thoughtful. You'd be surprised how far a little online courtesy can go.

#3 Privacy, Please!

It might be tempting to share every minute detail of your life online, but remember, some things are better left private. Check your privacy settings, and think before you post. Does the whole world need to know about that spat with your BFF or the details of your last breakup? Probably not.

#4 Spread Positivity

Use your online presence as a force for good. Share uplifting content, support causes you care about, and spread positivity. It can be as simple as posting a beautiful picture with an inspiring quote or encouraging someone who's going through a rough time. The internet can be a dark place sometimes, so why not light it up a bit?

#5 Digital Detox

Remember our talk about a social media detox? Don't be afraid to step away from your screens every now and then. It's okay to disconnect. Trust me, your followers won't forget you after a few days of silence. Plus, taking breaks can help you come back with fresh ideas and perspectives.

Creating a positive online presence isn't just about crafting a perfect image. It's about being your authentic, wonderful self and using your digital platform to inspire, uplift, and connect. Your social media profiles can be a window to your soul, so why not make the view beautiful? After all, this is the story of your life. Make sure it's one you're proud to share.

Chapter 12:

Sexual Health: More Than Just the "Talk"

The Birds, Bees, and Everything In-Between: Safe Sex Education

Okay, queen, let's have a real talk. No, not THE talk. We've all had that already. And if your experience was anything like mine, it was painfully awkward and probably left you with more questions than answers. So, let's dive in together into this world of safe sex education, without the blushing or stuttering!

1. Knowledge is Power

You've probably heard this so often it sounds like a cliché. But when it comes to sexual health, nothing could be truer. You need to understand your body, your options, and the risks involved with sexual activities. So get comfortable with terms like contraception, STDs, consent, and menstrual cycles. Yes, these words might make you squirm a little, but they're the ABCs of your sexual health.

2. Contraception - Not Just a Word in the Dictionary

Contraception is not just a fancy term you'll never use. It's your BFF when it comes to sexual health. There are so many options available - condoms, birth control pills, intrauterine devices (IUDs), implants, the list goes on. And remember, it's not just about preventing pregnancy, but also about protecting against sexually transmitted diseases (STDs).

3. Check-ups are your New Check-ins

Regular visits to your healthcare provider or gynecologist aren't something to be dreaded. They're as important as your daily skincare routine. Remember, prevention is better than cure, and that applies to your sexual health as well. Keep an eye on any changes and don't shy away from discussing them with your doctor.

4. No Means No

This one's important, girls. Consent is not negotiable. It's a fundamental right. You always have the power to say 'yes' or 'no', and you should never feel pressured into doing anything you're not comfortable with. Similarly, respect your partner's boundaries too. If they say 'no' or even 'maybe', take it as a 'no'. Consent should always be enthusiastic and mutual.

5. Myths? Bye, Felicia!

There are so many myths floating around about sex, it's like we're back in the age of Greek mythology. "You can't get pregnant on your first time." False. "You can't catch an STD if you're in a monogamous relationship." Also false. Make sure you're getting your information from reliable sources and not from the gossip mill.

Safe sex education isn't about scaremongering or creating taboos. It's about equipping you with the knowledge and tools you need to make informed decisions about your body. Remember, your sexual health is just as important as any other aspect of your health. So don't be afraid to ask questions, do your research, and take control. You've got this, girl!

Consent is Sexy: Understanding Boundaries

If you've ever thought that clear communication about consent could be a mood killer, think again. In fact, it's actually a green light for mutual respect, trust, and intimacy. To put it simply, consent is a complete, enthusiastic, and informed agreement between all parties involved in a sexual encounter. And let me tell you something: It's not only important, it's sexy. So let's break it down!

1. The Three Cs of Consent: Clear, Coherent, and Consistent

Just like your favorite online shopping site, consent needs to be clear, coherent, and consistent. No 'fine print' allowed! Clear means everyone involved knows exactly what they're agreeing to. Coherent means everyone is in a state where they can make an informed decision (so no, alcohol or drugs don't mix well with consent). And consistent means that consent can be given or withdrawn at any time, and that consent to one thing doesn't imply consent to anything else.

2. "But They Didn't Say No"

While we're on the topic, let's clear up a popular misconception. The absence of a 'no' doesn't equal a 'yes'. Consent isn't a game of hide-and-seek where you're trying to find the 'no' amidst the silence. It's the other way around - you're looking for a confident and enthusiastic 'yes'. And if it's not there, that's a no-go.

3. Consent is a Conversation

Discussing boundaries doesn't have to be a mood killer - in fact, it can be the opposite! Open and honest conversations about what you're comfortable with not only builds trust, but it also opens up a whole new world of understanding between you and your partner. It's a win-win!

4. Body Language Matters

Remember, consent isn't just verbal. Body language plays a crucial role in communication too. So, be attentive to your partner's non-verbal cues. If they tense up, pull away, or just don't seem as into it as you, that's a sign to stop and check-in verbally.

5. It's Okay to Change Your Mind

You ordered a strawberry milkshake, but when it arrived, you realized you really wanted chocolate. It happens! And just like with that milkshake, it's okay to change your mind about a sexual situation, too. You can always withdraw consent, and you owe it to yourself and your partner to communicate that change.

6. Respecting Boundaries

In the end, it's all about respect. Respecting your partner's boundaries is a sign of respect for them as a person, and it's a crucial part of any healthy relationship. Remember, anyone who truly cares about you will respect your boundaries, no questions asked.

To sum it up, consent is sexy, it's important, and it's a non-negotiable part of any sexual encounter. Understanding and practicing consent will help you build healthier relationships, while also ensuring that your boundaries and the boundaries of your partner are always respected. Go ahead, chica, have that conversation!

STDs, Screenings, and Prevention: Keeping It Safe

Alright, girly, it's time for some real talk: STDs. Yes, I know, the acronym itself is enough to give anyone the heebie-jeebies. But here's the thing, knowing about STDs (Sexually Transmitted Diseases), or as they're more fashionably known now, STIs (Sexually Transmitted Infections), is an absolute must-do in the game of life. So, let's get down to it!

1. Know Your ABCs...and STDs

Okay, so you probably know your ABCs backward and forward, but how about your STDs? And no, I'm not suggesting you recite them in alphabetical order (although, props to you if you can). I'm talking about understanding what they are, how they're transmitted, and their symptoms. Don't worry; you don't need to be a medical student. But knowing the basics? That's a must.

2. The Invisible Invaders

The freaky thing about many STDs is that they can be invisible. You can't necessarily tell by looking at someone if they have an STD, and even if you have an STD, you might not have any symptoms. Talk about an undercover operation! That's why it's so important to...

3. ... Get Tested, Stay Tested

So, let's imagine you're at a cute thrift shop, and you find a killer vintage tee. You wouldn't buy it without trying it on, right? Consider STD testing as trying on that vintage tee, but with higher stakes. Regular screenings are the only way to be sure you don't have an STD. And remember, testing isn't a one-and-done deal; it's an ongoing part of being sexually active.

4. Protection, Protection, Protection

No, that wasn't a typo. It's important enough to say three times. Using condoms is crucial for preventing the spread of most STDs. They're like the superheroes of safe sex, swooping in to protect you from unwanted pregnancies and those invisible invaders. And for an extra layer of protection, consider getting vaccinated for Hepatitis B and HPV (Human Papillomavirus) if you haven't already.

5. Let's Talk About It

Discussing STDs with a potential partner might feel about as comfortable as a porcupine in a balloon shop, but it's a conversation you need to have. Open dialogue about sexual health is a sign of respect and care for each other's well-being. And if someone isn't up for that convo, well, that's a red flag flapping in the wind.

6. And Remember...

Taking care of your sexual health is your responsibility. It's part of taking care of your overall health, just like brushing your teeth or getting that cardio in. No one else is going to do it for you (and honestly, would you want them to?).

So there you have it. STDs might be a buzzkill, but they're a part of life we can't ignore. But with knowledge, regular screenings, protection, and open conversations, we can keep ourselves and our partners safe. And that, my friend, is always in style.

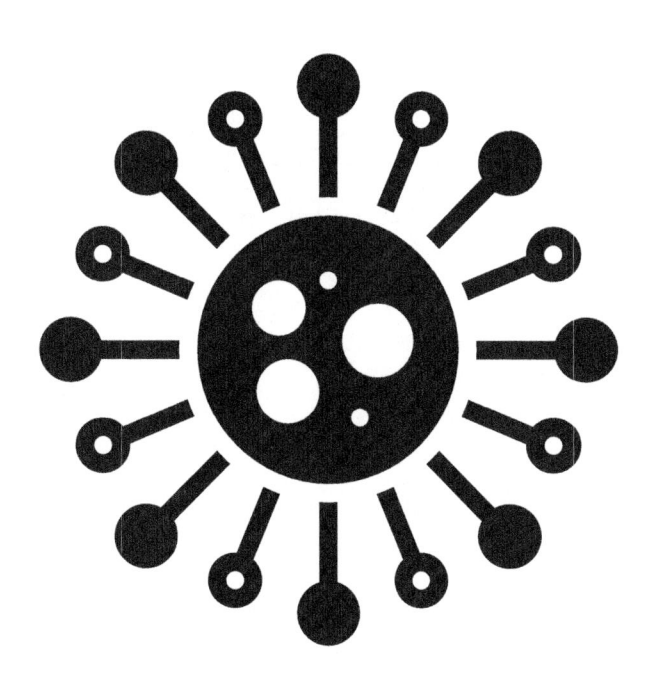

Healthy Relationships and Communication: Nurturing Intimacy

Lights, camera, action! Welcome to the scene of 'Healthy Relationships and Communication' where we ditch the script and get real about nurturing intimacy. We're not just talking the romantic, candlelit dinners type of intimacy, but the kind that involves open, honest, and raw communication.

1. The Emotional Roller Coaster

Relationships, my dear, can feel like riding a roller coaster. One moment, you're soaring, heart thumping, wind in your hair; the next, you're plummeting down at breakneck speed. But the ups and downs don't necessarily mean your relationship is on the fritz. It's all part of the ride, and having open and honest communication can turn that scary roller coaster into an exhilarating adventure.

2. The Talk that Walks the Walk

Now, I get it, having "the talk" can feel more daunting than being on stage at a karaoke night and forgetting the lyrics. But guess what? It doesn't have to be. Clear, consistent communication is like a magical potion for healthy relationships. It's about saying what you mean, meaning what you say, but don't say it mean— remember, it's not just about being heard, but also understanding your partner.

3. Unmasking the Intimacy Imposter

Physical attraction is like the flashy trailer for a movie—it draws you in. But remember, it's just the preview. Real intimacy is the whole film, complete with complex characters, plot twists, and emotional depth. It's about sharing experiences, dreams, fears, and yes, sometimes even your Netflix password. So, don't let the imposter steal the show!

4. The Art of Listening

Have you ever been in a conversation where you feel like you're just waiting for your turn to speak? Yeah, we've all been there. But true communication involves more listening than talking. Think of it like this: you have two ears and one mouth, so you should listen twice as much as you speak. Simple math, right?

5. Red Flags: Spotting the Bad Apples

In the grand garden of life, not everyone is going to be a sweet peach. Some might be rotten apples. Warning signs can include someone who disrespects you, pressures you, or makes you feel uncomfortable. These red flags are the universe's way of saying, "girl, you deserve better." Always trust your instincts.

6. You Do You

Remember, at the end of the day, the most important relationship is the one with yourself. Whether you're single, dating, or in a committed relationship, never lose sight of who you are and what you want. Your dreams, ambitions, and happiness should never take a back seat.

So there you have it. Relationships can be messy, complicated, and sometimes even a bit scary. But with a dash of communication, a sprinkle of understanding, and a whole lot of love (especially for yourself), you can navigate the world of intimacy with confidence. And remember, it's not about finding the perfect person, but loving the imperfect person perfectly. Now that's what I call a happily ever after!

Exploring Your Sexual Identity: Embracing Diversity and Self-Discovery

Gather round, queen! It's time to dive into the marvelous maze of sexuality and self-discovery. We're skipping the awkward classroom sex-ed talk and getting real about exploring your sexual identity. Grab a cup of hot cocoa, snuggle into your favorite reading spot, and let's set off on this empowering journey!

1. Unraveling the Rainbow

Sexual orientation isn't just black and white–it's a splendid rainbow of experiences and identities. Straight, gay, bisexual, pansexual, asexual, or somewhere in-between–there's a wide spectrum out there. It's like Baskin-Robbins's 31 flavors, but instead of ice cream, it's all the ways you could identify your sexuality. No matter where you land on this spectrum, your identity is valid, beautiful, and wholly yours.

2. The Sherlock Holmes Approach

Discovering your sexual identity can feel like you're the star of your own detective movie. Clues can appear in your attractions, emotions, or even dreams. You might find yourself drawn to boys, girls, both, or neither–and that's completely okay! Remember, everyone's timeline for this mystery is unique, so don't stress if your friends seem to be solving their case faster.

3. Facing Fear with Fierceness

Coming to terms with your sexuality can be scary—like watching a horror movie alone in the dark scary. It's normal to feel anxious, uncertain, or even scared. You might worry about being judged or not accepted. But let's flip the script and embrace that fear with a touch of fierceness. This is YOUR journey, YOUR truth, and it's nothing to be ashamed of.

4. Coming Out, or Staying In

The metaphorical closet can be a tough place to be. Coming out is a deeply personal decision and should happen on your terms and in your timing. It's not a one-size-fits-all situation, but more like finding the perfect prom dress—it takes time, patience, and you're the only one who can decide when and where it fits right.

5. Love is Love is Love

Regardless of how you identify, remember this golden rule: Love is love. It's about the connection between hearts, not the label of your sexual orientation. Whether you're crushing on the cute boy next door, the trendy girl in your art class, or anyone in between, what matters is how they treat you and how you feel about them.

6. Resources and Support

When you're exploring your sexual identity, it helps to have a map. This can come from books, blogs, videos, or organizations that offer information and support. Reach out to LGBT+ communities, both online and in real life. They can be like a GPS, guiding you through your self-discovery journey, providing valuable insights, and reminding you that you're not alone.

7. Staying True to You

Ultimately, the goal of exploring your sexual identity is to embrace your authentic self. It's about unraveling who you are, what you desire, and who you love. It's a journey of self-discovery that unfolds at your own pace, just like a butterfly emerging from a chrysalis.

Sexuality is a colorful and complex part of who you are, and exploring it is a courageous act of self-discovery. Remember, there's no right or wrong way to be you, and no matter where your journey leads, you're a unique, fierce, and fabulous individual. Stand tall, be proud, and always remember to love who you love and be who you are! Now, isn't that liberating?

Mental and Emotional Well-being: Addressing the Psychological Aspects of Sexual Health

Okay, so, we've talked about the physical stuff, the "do's and don'ts," the good, bad, and awkward of sexual health. But now, let's delve into the world of emotions, feelings, and mental health that's intertwined with our sexual selves. We're hopping on the roller coaster of the heart and mind, so strap yourself in!

1. Let's Get Emotional

Sexuality and emotional health go hand in hand like a romantic movie couple. When it comes to sexual experiences, our feelings often play the leading role, whether it's the bliss of a first kiss, the heartbreak of a breakup, or the anxiety of a sexual encounter. These emotional aspects are every bit as crucial as the physical ones.

2. But What Will People Think?

Worrying about others' opinions can sometimes feel like you're on an episode of "Reality TV Show: My Personal Life Edition." But remember, your sexual health and decisions are about YOU. You're the director of your own show, and it's okay to switch off those outside voices and focus on your own script. Let's say it together: "My body, my rules!"

3. The Joy of Consent

Yes, we're talking about consent again, and we'll keep on talking about it, like your favorite tune on repeat! Consent is crucial, not only for physical safety but for your mental health too. Feeling respected, heard, and safe is like a warm cup of hot chocolate for your mind.

4. Shame, Be Gone!

Sometimes, sexual thoughts and experiences can bring along a gloomy little cloud of shame or guilt. But honey, this isn't a 16th-century period drama, and you are NOT a damsel in distress. Recognize these feelings, question where they come from, and challenge them. Remember, there's no place for shame in your beautiful journey of self-discovery.

5. Relationship Stress: The Unwanted Guest

Even the best relationships come with a side dish of stress now and then. It's like ordering a delicious sundae and finding it's topped with pickles – not what you signed up for, right? Address this stress by talking to your partner, practicing self-care, and seeking professional help if needed. Remember, your mental health deserves priority seating at the table.

6. Healing After Heartbreak

Breakups can feel like your heart decided to run a marathon

without consulting you. Healing takes time, a pinch of self-love, and a dash of support from your friends and family. So put on that cozy sweater, watch your favorite movie, and let yourself heal. It's okay to feel the pain, but remember, you're stronger than you think.

7. Seek Support

Just like how you wouldn't hesitate to see a doctor for a broken arm, seeking help for emotional distress is perfectly normal. Whether it's from a psychologist, therapist, counselor, or a trusted person in your life, there's never any shame in reaching out.

Sexual health isn't just about knowing the ins and outs of the physical act itself. It's about understanding and nurturing your mental and emotional wellbeing too. And always remember, no matter what you're going through, you're a dazzling star in the infinite galaxy of womanhood, and there's a whole universe of support out there for you!

Chapter 13:

Career Planning: Chase the Dream, Not the Money

Finding Your Passion:
The Job vs Career Debate

Picture this: you're on your favorite show, 'Life Choices', and the host presents you with two doors. Behind door number one is a 'job'. Behind door number two, a 'career'. What's the difference? It feels like the same thing, right? They both involve work, they both pay, and you probably need a resume for both. But hold onto your high heels, because we're about to dive deeper!

You see, a 'job' is like your summer fling - it's a fun experience, it pays for your new clothes, but you're probably not going to marry it. It's what you do for a while, until you find 'the one'. A 'career', on the other hand, is like your true love. It's that long-term commitment that you nurture and grow over time. It's what makes your heart flutter every morning (well, most mornings) as you get out of bed and think, "I'm going to conquer the world today!"

Now, choosing between a job and a career isn't like picking out your prom dress. It's not a one-time thing, but more like trying on different outfits until you find the one that fits just right. And let's face it, who doesn't love trying on new clothes?

Passion. Oh, that elusive beast! Many a philosopher and career coach have waxed eloquent about 'following your passion'. But, let's toss that cliché out the window for a moment. Here's the thing: it's not about following your passion as much as it's about nurturing and cultivating it. If you don't know what you're passionate about yet, that's okay! It's like finding that perfect shade of lipstick - it takes a bit of trial and error. Keep experimenting and remain open to new experiences.

Your first job may not seem like a dream come true, and you might feel more like Cinderella before the ball rather than after. And that's perfectly okay. Just remember that Cinderella didn't just sit around waiting for her fairy godmother, she went out there and made things happen! Your first job is an opportunity to learn, grow, and discover what you enjoy and what you're good at. It might not be your dream job, but it will definitely help you figure out what your dream job might be.

Remember, at the end of the day, the most stylish thing you can wear is confidence, and the most beautiful thing you can do is chase your dreams. Whether it's a job or a career, embrace the opportunity, learn as much as you can, and let your experiences guide you towards your passion. Now, go rock that world, girl!

Internships, Resumes, and Interviews: The Basics

Think of your career journey like the most epic fashion show ever. You start with the behind-the-scenes hustle - the internships. Then comes the glittering display - your resume. And finally, the big reveal - the interview. Now, let's dive into this fabulous world and sashay down the career runway, shall we?

Let's talk internships first. They're like those trendy clothes you try on in the fitting room - some fit you perfectly, some don't, but each piece gives you a little more insight into what you love and what suits you. Internships provide you with real-world experience and a glimpse into what your future career might look like. Some days might feel like you're just fetching coffee and photocopying papers (or the virtual equivalent if you're interning from home). But even then, you're learning - about the work environment, about dealing with people, about handling responsibility, and about turning coffee into survival juice (kidding, sort of).

Next up is the resume, the outfit that you'd wear to the career catwalk. You want it to be a show-stopper, right? Just like you wouldn't wear a hodgepodge of styles to a fashion event, your resume should be concise, coherent, and well-structured. It's your career's Little Black Dress, if you will. Include your educational background, work experiences, skills, and accomplishments. But remember, just like an overly shiny sequined dress, you don't want your resume to be cluttered. So, no need to mention that you won a pie-eating contest when you were 12 unless, of course, you're applying to be a pie tester. Now, wouldn't that be a dream?

Okay, time for the spotlight moment - the interview. Imagine strutting down the runway. The lights are bright, your heart's pounding, and the music's just right. You know you've got to give it your all. Well, that's what an interview feels like. And just like you wouldn't show up to the fashion week in your cozy pyjamas, you wouldn't show up to an interview unprepared. Know about the company, the role, and how your skills match. Be ready to answer common questions and also to ask a few of your own. An interview is not just about them getting to know you; it's also about you getting to know them.

Remember, in this grand fashion show of life, internships, resumes, and interviews are your stepping stones. They might seem intimidating, but they're your golden tickets to the backstage of your dream career. So, go ahead, girl! Dress up, show up, and light up that runway with your brilliance!

The Hustle:
Managing Stress in the Workplace

Welcome to the adulting rollercoaster where juggling job demands with your mental wellbeing can feel like walking a tightrope... blindfolded... with squirrels throwing acorns at you. Yep, it's the good ol' workplace stress, the unwelcome friend we never asked for, yet always seems to show up uninvited. Let's dive into some tips and tricks to navigate this labyrinth of deadlines, meetings, and office dramas.

Let's start with your workspace. Remember that time when you thought your room was a black hole, only to discover your missing earring under a pile of clothes after a cleanup? Similarly, a chaotic workspace can often mirror and amplify your internal stress. So, let's Marie Kondo it. Keep your space tidy, organized, and filled with items that 'spark joy'. Maybe it's a cute plant (cacti for the win, they're hard to kill!), photos of your dog, or even just a fancy pen. Little things can often create a soothing environment.

Next, the age-old advice that's as relevant as a Lizzo bop in a party playlist – take breaks. I know, your schedule seems busier than Times Square on New Year's Eve. But remember, even the brightest star needs a moment away from shining. Short breaks can help you stay productive without burning out. Maybe do a quick yoga stretch, take a mini dance party break, or just look away from the screen and enjoy a few sips of your unicorn tears infused frappe-latte-mochaccino. Your brain will thank you later.

Let's not forget the magical power of communication. When you're feeling swamped, talking about it can be as relieving as taking off high heels after a long night. So, whether it's with a coworker, a manager, or your pet tarantula, don't be afraid to express your concerns. You might be surprised at how much support you can get, and, if you're talking to the tarantula, how good it can be to just vent.

Also, while we're discussing stress, let's acknowledge the elephant in the room: the need to strive for perfection. It's like trying to make an Instagrammable breakfast every morning - beautiful but time-consuming and not necessary. Know that it's okay to have 'off' days. We all have them, despite what your Instagram feed might have you believe. So, try to be as kind to yourself as you would be to your best friend.

Finally, the most important weapon in your stress-busting arsenal: self-care. Remember that you're a beautiful orchid that needs watering (or, you know, a cactus if you've been forgetting the watering part). Incorporate activities you love into your routine - be it a dance class, painting, or that guilty pleasure reality show. It's about giving your mind a break and letting it have some fun.

In the words of the phenomenal Dory, "just keep swimming." Stress may seem like a relentless wave, but with these tips, you'll be surfing in no time. So, keep on shining, hustling, and being the fabulous girl you are. Because at the end of the day, you're not just chasing a career, you're building a life. So make it a good one!

Chapter 14:

Adulting 101:
The Stuff They Don't Teach You

Bills, Taxes, and Insurance: The Basics

Buckle up, queen! We're about to venture into the dark and mystifying labyrinth of adulting. No, it's not an episode of "Stranger Things", it's the mind-boggling world of bills, taxes, and insurance! While it might not be as flashy as a Coachella concert, conquering these essentials will have you feeling like Beyonce at the Superbowl!

First stop, bills. They may be as annoying as a pop-up ad in the middle of your favorite YouTube video, but they are as inevitable as your obsession with everything Harry Styles. There's your phone bill, electricity, water, rent, and that streaming service bill (because who can live without their weekly dose of K-dramas?). Don't be overwhelmed, though. Just like organizing your makeup, it's all about setting up a system.

First, keep track of your monthly bills, maybe use a budgeting app (we live in the era of technology, after all). Ensure you know when every bill is due. Forgetting a bill due date can have you scrambling like it's the last item on sale at Sephora. If you can, set up auto-payments. You know, like how your phone automatically corrects "omw" to "On my way!" because it somehow knows you're always running late.

Next up, taxes, the 'Thanos' of adulting. They are confusing and can seem like they want to destroy your happiness, but understanding them is crucial. Taxes pay for important stuff like roads, schools, and healthcare. Your employer will typically deduct this from your paycheck (that's why your take-home pay looks slimmer than the number you were initially promised). You'll need to file a tax return every year, which is basically like Instagram – you report your 'earnings' (income), claim your 'filters' (deductions and credits) and then see if you've paid enough likes (taxes). If you've paid too much, you get a refund (woohoo!). If not, you'll have to pay the difference (*cue sad trombone*). It might seem daunting, but there are plenty of free resources and inexpensive software to help you out.

And finally, we have the unsung hero of adulting, insurance. It's like that umbrella you forgot you had until it started raining, and you were oh so thankful for it. Whether it's health, car, or renter's insurance, it provides a financial safety net. You pay a small amount regularly, so if something bad happens (like a car accident or medical issue), your insurance steps in to cover most of the costs. It's like buying peace of mind in installments.

Dealing with bills, taxes, and insurance can initially feel like trying to follow a James Charles makeup tutorial with no makeup experience – a little scary, pretty complicated, and with a high chance of mistakes. But, remember, you're not expected to know it all instantly. You're learning. Give yourself time, ask for help when you need it, and gradually, it will start making sense. Or at the very least, it will become a part of your routine, just like your nightly skincare regimen!

And who knows? You might just find yourself someday, cup of coffee in hand, flipping through tax forms, and paying your bills on time, thinking, "Look at me, adulting like a boss." Because, girl, you got this!

Cooking, Cleaning, Laundry: Domestic Goddesses in the Making

Pop the confetti, because it's time to channel your inner goddess – your Domestic Goddess, that is! Before you groan and consider surviving on takeout for the rest of your life, hear me out. I know the idea of cooking, cleaning, and doing laundry seems as appealing as being stuck in an elevator with a bunch of people who just did an intense hot-yoga session (eeew!), but let's make it fun and fabulous, shall we?

Cooking – Your Experimental Studio

First off, cooking! It's not just about feeding yourself (although that is a pretty big perk). It's an art, a dance, a science experiment, and the ultimate self-care rolled into one. Plus, you can go from "I can burn water" to "Watch me whip up this pasta alla vodka" quicker than you can say "TikTok viral recipe"!

The trick? Start small. Think about some of your favorite dishes and look for easy recipes online. Cooking is just following instructions, and with the internet at our fingertips, even the most complicated dishes come with step-by-step guides, often with pictures and videos. Remember when you learned the Renegade dance from that slow-mo tutorial? Same thing, but this time, you'll be rewarded with a delicious meal!

Cleaning – No, Not the Chore

Next up, cleaning! I know, you're thinking, "Cleaning? Really? This is worse than that time they killed off my favorite character on 'Riverdale'." But let's try to change the narrative. Don't think of it as a chore but as a feel-good activity. Think about it, nothing beats the satisfaction of a clean room that smells of fresh linen, right? It's like living in your very own Pinterest board.

Instead of tackling everything at once, break it down. Create a little cleaning schedule (nothing fancy, a sticky note will do), assign one area or task for each day. And hey, crank up that Spotify playlist and make it a groove-clean session. Dancing around with a vacuum cleaner pretending it's a duet with Harry Styles? Yes, please!

Laundry – Wash, Dry, Fold, Repeat (Kinda)

Now, we're onto laundry. It might seem like a never-ending cycle (pun intended) but it doesn't have to be your nemesis. Laundry is like that old game of Tetris, trying to fit different clothes into the machine effectively, managing colors and fabrics, and trying to decipher those hieroglyphics they call laundry symbols. It's an adventure, and who doesn't love a good adventure?

Just remember the basics: separate your whites from your colored clothes, delicates get their special treatment (because they're the divas of your wardrobe), and always check your pockets unless you want a snowfall of tissue pieces on your clothes.

Finally, folding. It's like yoga for your clothes. It can be therapeutic, almost meditative. And if you think about it, it's pretty cool that there are so many ways to fold a T-shirt or pair of socks. And if all else fails, there's always the option of rolling clothes – it saves space and reduces wrinkles!

Mastering these domestic skills is like leveling up in a video game. It might be hard at first, and you may wish you could hit the "skip" button. But as you learn and grow, you'll unlock new achievements and powers you never knew you had. So, girl, let's grab this adulting thing by the horns and become the Domestic Goddesses we're destined to be! Because, who run the world? GIRLS!

Time Management: Work, Life, and Play

Oh, to have Hermione Granger's Time-Turner. Imagine the joy of being able to attend two classes simultaneously, grab a coffee with a friend, while also managing to squeeze in a Quidditch match! Alas, here in the Muggle world, time-turners are sadly not an option. However, as Dumbledore wisely said, "It is our choices that show what we truly are, far more than our abilities," and that absolutely applies to managing our time.

Let's break it down, sprinkle in some magic dust (sadly, just metaphorical), and see how we can balance work, life, and play without needing to attend Hogwarts.

Work – Do What You Gotta Do

Yes, we all gotta work. Whether you're at school, in college, or at a job, this is the part of your day where you might feel you're transforming into a productivity robot. The solution? Break it down! Set clear goals for each day, keep it realistic, and prioritize. It's like trying to fit your entire wardrobe into a suitcase. You can't bring everything, so you bring what's important. In work, too, tackle the significant tasks first (the jeans and jackets of your suitcase), and then, if there's time, deal with the smaller, less urgent tasks (the socks and scarves).

Now, what if your to-do list is as long as Rapunzel's hair? The trick is to break it up into manageable chunks. We call it the Pomodoro Technique, but let's rename it the TikTok Technique, where you dedicate 25 minutes (approximately the length of 8 TikToks) to focused work, then take a 5-minute break (just enough time to watch 2 more TikToks). This technique keeps you focused and gives your brain some well-deserved breaks.

Life – Let's Get Real

We are so much more than just students or employees. We're friends, daughters, sisters, hobbyists, aspiring TikTok dancers, and sometimes, we just want to be a couch potato and binge-watch 'Stranger Things'. That's where life comes in.

Life activities include taking care of your mental and physical health, connecting with your family and friends, and pursuing hobbies. It's like making a great smoothie bowl. You need a bit of everything for a well-rounded life – a splash of yoga, a sprinkle of chit-chat with your bestie, and a handful of your favorite hobby. Just as no two smoothie bowls are alike, no two 'life' recipes will be the same. Customize it to what makes you feel good!

Play – Fun is Serious Business

Now, let's talk about play. This is your time to let loose, watch those YouTube tutorials on the latest dance moves, create elaborate stories on 'The Sims', or just hang out and laugh with friends. It's important to remember that 'play' isn't frivolous. It's just as important as work and life. Consider it like the cherry on top of your cake – not a necessity, but oh boy, does it make the cake a whole lot better!

Balancing work, life, and play is more of an art than a science. The key is to remember that it's okay if things don't go perfectly. Some days, your work will spill into your life. Other days, you'll find yourself binge-watching a Netflix series when you should be working. And that's okay. Remember that we're not striving for perfection, but balance. We're all trying to figure it out, one TikTok, one assignment, and one smoothie bowl at a time. Because if adulting has taught us anything, it's that we're all winging it, and that's perfectly okay. Now go out there and slay, girl!

Chapter 15:

Substance Use: Knowing the Risks

Alcohol and Drugs:
The Reality Beyond the Party

Oh, the fabled party scene. You know, the one you've seen in almost every teen movie ever. The one with red solo cups, dancing around a bonfire, or chilling in someone's basement turned nightclub. The cool kids are doing shots, there's smoke hovering in the air, and the scene looks as if it came straight out of a music video. It might look fun and glamorous, but let's be real, it's not all glitter and stilettos. Let's go backstage, where the mascara is smudged, and the music is too loud.

Alcohol and drugs, huh? Let's call them the "bad boys" of the party. They seem all mysterious and exciting, but remember, much like dating a bad boy, there can be consequences, and they're not usually the good kind.

Alcohol: Not Just a Red Solo Cup

It might be the life of the party, but much like the life of a party, alcohol can be unpredictable, and sometimes, a bit of a hot mess. We're not here to be the fun police, but rather the fun's best friend, who makes sure it's home safe.

Alcohol, when consumed in moderation, can be a part of socializing. But remember the golden rule, babe: Know. Your. Limits. You wouldn't eat an entire pizza, a tub of ice cream, and a mountain of fries in one sitting, right? The same logic applies to alcohol. Overdoing it can lead to consequences that are as unpleasant as a food coma - only worse. It can lead to risky behavior, health problems, and let's not forget, those cringe-worthy hangovers.

Drugs: Smoke and Mirrors

Now, let's talk about the other elephant in the room: drugs. They might seem like the key to coolness or an escape hatch from reality. But lady, that's the grand illusion. It's all smoke and mirrors, and the truth is far from the fantasy. Drugs can and do wreak havoc on your health, ambitions, and relationships. Remember, the temporary high is not worth the long-term low.

We're not just talking about the "hard stuff" here. Even the "green goddess" marijuana, often seen as a chill-out tool, can have serious consequences, especially for us young adults. Studies have shown that it can affect our brain development, which is still ongoing until our mid-20s (who knew, right?).

The Bottom Line

It's essential to be informed about the risks and make choices that are right for you. Peer pressure can be a tough cookie to handle, but remember, you're the queen of your own life. Don't let the "you only live once" mentality bully you into making decisions you're not comfortable with.

At the end of the day, you want your party scene to be more

"dance-off" and less "dance with danger." As the old saying goes, it's better to be safe than sorry. Make sure your fun stays fun, and doesn't turn into a cautionary tale.

So, party on, girl! But remember, the real party is living your best life, and for that, you need to take care of yourself. In the words of Beyoncé, "I dream it, I work hard, I grind 'til I own it." And, if I may add, I take care of my health while I'm at it! Keep the Beyoncé spirit in you alive and let it guide you through your epic journey! Slay, girl! Slay!

trust your **JOURNEY**

Understanding Addiction: When Fun Becomes Fatal

Oh honey, don't we all just love a good binge? Netflix, cookie dough ice cream, shopping...you name it. But what happens when that "fun" binge escalates into a full-blown addiction? Suddenly, it's not about 12 episodes of Stranger Things in one night (we've all been there); it's about something far more sinister and seriously not cool.

Let's step into this not-so-fabulous world of addiction for a moment, shall we?

Addiction: Not A VIP Club You Want to Join

In the simplest terms, addiction is like having that annoying song stuck in your head, but instead of a catchy tune, it's a substance or behavior that you can't stop thinking about. It's like being on a rollercoaster ride that you can't get off, even though you're feeling sick and the fun is long gone.

And the bouncer in this club doesn't care how cute you look in your little black dress; addiction does not discriminate. It can grab anyone, at any age, in any circumstance. It's sneaky like that. It might start as something casual - a drink here, a smoke there - but then it slowly escalates until you're in way over your head.

Addiction - The Drama Queen of the Brain

Addiction is the ultimate drama queen. It demands your attention, hijacks your life, and won't let go. It's like that mean girl from high school who wants everything her way. Except, in this case, the mean girl is inside your brain.

When you're addicted, your brain is basically having a meltdown. It's no longer about wanting the substance; it's about needing it. Addiction alters the brain's structure and function, leading to changes that stick around long after you stop using the substance.

Rehab: The Real-Life Makeover Show

Rehabilitation or 'rehab' for short, might not be as glamorous as the makeovers in reality shows, but trust me, it's way more empowering. Imagine it as a journey, with the road sometimes bumpy, sometimes smooth, but always leading to a better place.

Rehab is not just about quitting; it's about understanding why you started in the first place. It's about learning new ways to cope with stress, rebuild relationships, and nurture your mental health. It's about reclaiming your life, one step at a time.

Your Life: The Best Show On The Planet

Remember, babes, you are not a passive viewer in your life. You are the main character, the heroine, the boss lady. This is your show, and you're the one calling the shots. If you or someone you know is struggling with addiction, don't hesitate to seek help.

Addiction might seem like a never-ending horror show, but the lights come on when you reach out for help. Remember, it's not about the fall, it's about the bounce back. Don't let addiction write your story. You're the author here, so pick up that pen and write a comeback that rocks!

So, let's wrap this up with a cheer, queen! Here's to understanding addiction, seeking help when needed, and most importantly, celebrating our journey - the highs, the lows, and everything in-between. Because remember, life is not a sprint; it's a marathon, and every step, no matter how small, is a step forward. And that, my darlings, is what truly matters!

Help and Support: Recovery is Possible

Girl, pull up a chair, grab your favorite flavored bubble tea, and let's have a chat. We've ventured through the dark corners of addiction, but now it's time to fling open those curtains and let in some much-needed light. Let's talk about something so important it could be a tagline in a superhero movie: Help and Support - because, darling, recovery is not just possible, it's inevitable!

Buckle Up For Your Journey to Recovery

Think of recovery as that challenging yet rewarding road trip where you're in the driver's seat. Sure, you might hit some traffic jams (read: challenges), and you might take a wrong turn or two (read: relapses), but hey, that's part of the journey. The destination - your best, healthiest self - is totally worth it!

So, let's fasten our seatbelts, adjust our rear-view mirrors, and rev up the engines. It's time to drive towards recovery with an awesome playlist on and a strong support system in the backseat!

The Lifelines in Your Game of Recovery

You know how in those game shows, there's always a lifeline you can use when you're stuck? Well, honey, in this game of recovery, you've got plenty of them! From therapists and counselors to support groups and hotlines, help is just a call (or a click) away.

Therapists and Counselors: Think of these folks as your personal navigators. They're trained professionals who can provide tools to help you cope with cravings and manage your life without the need for substances. And don't worry, they aren't going to judge you. Their goal is to help you reach yours!

Support Groups: Ever heard of the phrase, "There's strength in numbers"? Well, it couldn't be truer! Support groups are like those group study sessions back in high school, except here, you're learning about resilience and sharing experiences with others who truly get it.

Hotlines: Picture hotlines as your SOS beacons. They're available round-the-clock for when you need immediate help or just someone to talk to. So, remember, no matter how tough things get, there's always someone ready to pick up the call and lend an ear.

Empowerment: Your Secret Superpower

In this journey towards recovery, you're not just the main character; you're the superhero. And guess what your superpower is? It's empowerment. That's right, girl! When you're empowered, you're in control, you're strong, and you're ready to kick some serious butt.

Remember, you're not defined by your addiction. You're defined by how you rise from it, how you empower yourself, and how you help others. So, put on that cape, and show the world just how powerful you truly are!

The Art of Asking for Help

Now, let's be real, we all have moments where we're as stubborn as a mule and hate asking for help. But remember, asking for help doesn't make you weak, it makes you strong. It shows that you're brave enough to acknowledge you're struggling and smart enough to do something about it. So, never be shy about reaching out.

Let's wrap this up with a virtual high-five, queen! Here's to understanding the importance of help and support, to recognizing our strength, and to reminding ourselves that we are not alone. Recovery is not just possible; it's our reality waiting to happen!

Peer Pressure and Saying No: Navigating Social Situations

Alright, babe, it's time for a pop quiz! Picture this: you're at a party, the music's pumping, and the energy's infectious. A friend (or a friend of a friend, or a cute stranger you've just met) slides up to you and offers you a little something-something that you know isn't exactly the healthiest choice. What do you do? I hear you, it's easier to sing opera in front of a full auditorium than to utter that tiny but powerful word: NO. But let's break this down and put the 'peer' in 'peer pressure' under a microscope.

Being in the Spotlight Isn't Always Fabulous

Ah, the dreaded peer pressure - it's like being the star of a reality TV show you never auditioned for. Suddenly, you're the center of attention, and saying 'no' feels like breaking the unwritten script. But here's a little secret: most of the time, that spotlight is all in your head. People are too busy with their own lives to focus on your every decision. So, if you decide to skip the chugging contest or the joint rotation, it's likely people won't even notice or remember the next day. And if they do and make a fuss about it? Well, they don't deserve a spot in your VIP section.

The Art of Saying 'No'

Despite what we may have learned from romance novels, 'No' is a complete sentence. It doesn't require an explanation, an excuse, or a justification. Just a full stop. But we get it, sometimes, that 'no' can get stuck in your throat, like a piece of too-dry toast. So, here are some fabulous ways to say 'no' in style:

The Comedic No: Use humor to defuse the situation. "Me, drink that? I'd rather wrestle a bear!"
The Polite No: A simple "No, thank you" with a smile can work wonders.
The Direct No: Being straightforward can be surprisingly effective. "I don't do drugs."
Remember, you don't owe anyone a detailed explanation. It's your body, your life, and your rules.

The Power of the Right Crowd

Surround yourself with people who respect your boundaries and choices. These are the folks who won't push you into things you don't want to do, and they're your real MVPs. They're the kind of pals who would rather share a giant pizza or binge-watch the latest series with you than push you to the edge of your comfort zone.

Practice Makes Perfect

Just like perfecting your winged eyeliner or nailing that dance routine on TikTok, learning to say 'no' takes practice. It's like flexing a muscle. The more you do it, the easier it becomes. So flex that 'no' muscle, girl!

In the end, remember, true friends will respect your 'no,' and the rest, well, they're about as important as that 2007 meme you barely remember. You're strong, you're capable, and you have the power to navigate any social situation, even when it feels as challenging as a boss level in a video game. So game on, girl! We've got this!

Chapter 16:

Relationships with Parents: The Evolving Bond

From Dependence to Independence: Shifting Dynamics

Oh, parents. They can be the superheroes of our childhood, the villains of our teenage rebellion, and the strange mix of sidekick and sage in our adult lives. Navigating the changing dynamics as you shift from dependence to independence can feel like trying to walk straight after a whirl on a merry-go-round - disorienting, unpredictable, and occasionally nauseating. But fear not, darlings, because we're about to break down this complicated dance step by step.

Seeing the Cape for the First Time

You know that moment in superhero movies where the hero takes off their mask and reveals their true identity? Yeah, well, becoming an adult is a bit like that, but instead of Batman, you're dealing with your parents. It's realizing that they're not just 'mom' or 'dad', but individuals with their own dreams, fears, and flaws. Crazy, right? The process of becoming independent often involves seeing your parents in a new light, which can be as exciting as discovering a new TV show and as heartbreaking as the end of your favorite book series. But it's a part of growing up, just like outgrowing those beloved pair of shoes from two summers ago.

Navigating the Power Shift

The road to independence is a bit like a see-saw. On one end, you have your growing desire for freedom and autonomy. On the other end, your parents' instinct to protect and guide you. This can create a power shift that's as wobbly as a fawn learning to walk. But don't worry, girl, we've got you. Here are some tips to handle this:

Communication is Key: Open up about your feelings. Articulate your needs for independence, but also understand your parents' concerns.

Responsibility Check: Show them you're ready for independence by handling your responsibilities. Yes, even those pesky chores.

Negotiate and Compromise: Becoming independent doesn't mean winning every argument. It's about negotiation and compromise, like sharing that last slice of pizza with your sibling.

Setting Boundaries

Just as you wouldn't want your parents to barge into your room when you're in the middle of a killer dance routine, they may not want you to invade their space without knocking. Respect goes both ways, and it's okay to establish boundaries as you become more independent. Just remember to do it with kindness and understanding.

Adulthood: A Two-Way Street

Becoming an adult doesn't mean you have to give up needing your parents. It's like those old band t-shirts you can't bring yourself to throw away; they're always there, offering comfort and nostalgia. So, as you explore this new dynamic, remember that it's okay to lean on your parents. After all, independence isn't about doing everything alone - it's about knowing when to ask for help.

And remember, sweet girls, even as you fly the nest, you're not leaving your parents behind. You're simply inviting them to see a new side of you, the independent, strong woman you're becoming. And that's a show worth tuning into. So, here's to turning the page and starting this exciting new chapter! Let's do this!

Setting Boundaries with Parents: Navigating Disagreements

So, we've talked about the changing dynamics with parents as you inch towards adulthood. But let's be real, even superheroes disagree, right? I mean, remember the whole 'Civil War' thing with Iron Man and Captain America? Just like that, disagreements with parents are inevitable. But, don't worry. You don't need a superhero suit or vibranium shield to navigate these battles. So, buckle up, lady, as we dive into the sometimes-messy-but-always-necessary world of setting boundaries and navigating disagreements with parents.

The Art of 'No'

Saying 'no' to your parents can feel as daunting as wearing neon colors to a black and white party. You worry about standing out, being different, or causing a scene. But the truth is, 'no' is a complete sentence and it's a crucial part of setting boundaries. Here's a tip: practice in front of a mirror. It might seem silly, but trust me, seeing yourself say 'no' confidently can be empowering.

It's Not a Battlefield

Disagreements with parents can sometimes feel like you're at war, but remember, you're not enemies. You're on the same side! Disagreeing doesn't mean you stop loving each other. So, check your weapons at the door, girls. No need for hurtful words or personal attacks. Keep it civil and respect each other's feelings.

R-E-S-P-E-C-T

You might be singing it in your head right now, and that's cool because Aretha Franklin knew what she was talking about! Respect is key. You're an adult now, and that means you deserve to be heard. But remember, respect is a two-way street. You also need to respect your parents' opinions, even if you don't agree with them.

Communicate, Don't Complicate

You know when you're trying to assemble that IKEA furniture (yes, another IKEA reference, deal with it, missy) and the instructions are just NOT making sense? Well, a lack of clear communication with parents can feel like that. Don't just express your disagreement, explain why you feel that way. Let them into your thought process. Understanding each other's perspectives can go a long way in resolving disagreements.

Pick Your Battles

Not every disagreement needs to be a showdown. It's okay to let some things go. If your dad still calls your favorite band by the wrong name, maybe that's not worth a fight. But if something truly matters to you, stand your ground.

Calling in the Referee

Sometimes, a disagreement with parents can feel like you're in a deadlock. It's okay to seek help from an outside party. A trusted relative, a family counselor, or even a family friend can provide a fresh perspective and help mediate the discussion.

And there you have it, hot stuff! Remember, setting boundaries and navigating disagreements isn't about winning or losing. It's about understanding and respecting each other's space, feelings, and opinions. It's not always easy, but it's a dance worth learning. After all, life isn't a superhero movie, it's more like a musical - sometimes messy, sometimes harmonious, but always a spectacle worth being a part of. So here's to keeping the rhythm, even when the music changes.

Appreciating Family:
The Importance of Gratitude

Roll out the red carpet, girls, because it's time for the Academy Awards of Emotions: the 'Gratitude Gala'. Okay, okay, it might sound as cheesy as an extra cheese pizza, but hey, who doesn't love an extra cheese pizza?

Being grateful isn't about being the perfect 'Hallmark card' daughter, no one is expecting you to break into a 'Sound of Music' gratitude song every morning (although, if you did, I'm sure it would be a hit!). Gratitude is more like a comfy old t-shirt; it's soft, familiar, and always fits just right, even on the days when we feel like nothing else does.

The Gratitude Attitude

Being grateful is not just about saying 'thank you'. It's a way of seeing the world. It's like putting on a pair of magical glasses that let you see the good in everything. Yeah, even in that zit on your nose that decided to appear right before your big date, because hey, it gives you an excuse to try out that new concealer, right?

The Science Behind the Smiles

There's this thing called 'positive psychology'. It's like your brain's fairy godmother. It's been proven that focusing on gratitude can lead to better sleep, reduced stress, and even increased happiness.

If that doesn't motivate you to get your gratitude on, I don't know what will!

The Little Things

Gratitude isn't about only appreciating the big, shiny, Instagram-worthy moments. It's about finding joy in the simple, everyday things too. Like when your mom makes your favorite pancakes on a random Tuesday, or when your dad saves the last slice of pizza for you. These small acts of love are like the sequins on the dress of life; tiny, but they make everything sparkle.

Dear Diary

Gratitude journals are the latest 'it' thing, just like bell-bottom jeans in the '70s. Except, you won't look back at this in a few years and wonder 'what was I thinking?' Spend a few minutes each day jotting down things you're grateful for. It could be as simple as 'good hair day' or as deep as 'mom's advice about breakups'.

Say It Out Loud

Express your gratitude. Tell your parents you appreciate them. Write them a note, send them a text, or if you're feeling particularly brave, tag them in your social media post about gratitude (cue dramatic gasps).

Return the Favor

Showing gratitude isn't just about saying it, it's about showing it too. Cook a meal for your parents, take on an extra chore, or simply spend some time with them. Actions speak louder than words, after all.

Remember, queeny, family is like your favorite book. It's comforting, familiar, sometimes frustrating, and occasionally confusing. But, it's unique to you and it's a story worth cherishing. So, let's throw on those gratitude glasses and start seeing the magic in the everyday. Because, let's be real, who needs a fairy godmother when you have the power to transform your own world into a fairytale?

Chapter 17:

Self-Exploration: Discovering Your True Potential

Embracing Your Passions: Unleashing Your Creative Side

Hello, you beautiful soul explorer! Welcome aboard the express train to Self-Exploration City. Buckle up, because our first stop is the wildly exciting and endlessly colorful Creativity Land. So grab your passion paintbrushes, let's add some vibrant hues to this adventure!

Express Yourself, Don't Repress Yourself

When we talk about creativity, let's be clear: it's not about becoming the next Frida Kahlo or Beethoven (though if you are, hi, can I get your autograph?). It's about expressing yourself, and let me tell you, self-expression is as important as that Instagram-filtered selfie you took last week.

Why Creativity Matters

You know that joyful feeling when you're belting out your favorite tune in the shower, dancing like no one's watching, or doodling on your notebook during a boring class (Sorry, Mrs. Johnson)? That's your inner creative goddess breaking out. And trust me, she's more fun than a surprise text from your crush!

Finding Your Creative Outlet

Whether it's dancing in the rain or singing like a superstar using a hairbrush as your microphone, your creative outlet is like your very own magic spell, ready to turn every ordinary moment into an extraordinary one. Your passion could be anything: photography, fashion, cooking, writing, or even reorganizing your room for the zillionth time. It's your story, darling, you get to pick the genre!

Dear Society, My Creativity is Not Up for Debate

Ignore the critics (yes, even if one of them happens to be your judgmental Aunt Carol). There's no such thing as bad art or a lousy passion. The best part of creativity is that it's entirely, beautifully, and unapologetically yours.

Rome Wasn't Built in a Day, And Neither Are Your Skills

Remember when you first tried to walk? Me neither, but I'm pretty sure we all fell flat on our cute baby faces more than once. The point is, learning a new skill is like teaching a baby to walk; it takes time, patience, and a lot of funny falls. Embrace the mistakes and don't be afraid to fail. As the saying goes, 'mistakes are the stepping stones to success'... or in our case, creativity.

A Date With Creativity

Set aside some time for your passions. Call it your creative date. During this time, you are the boss. Want to paint your feelings? Go ahead. Feel like creating a new TikTok dance challenge? Show them your moves, girl!

Join The Club

Share your passions. Join a club, start a blog, or even host a small get-together with your friends to share your latest creations. Passion is contagious, and it only grows when shared!

So, my lovely explorer, let's dive into the ocean of creativity, make some waves, and find those hidden pearls of passion. Remember, in this journey of self-exploration, there are no speed limits, no wrong turns, and definitely no end to the creative road. So, get set, and unleash your creative side!

Setting Goals and Dreaming Big: Turning Ambitions into Reality

Alright, lady, it's time to navigate from the bright lands of creativity and plunge into the adventurous world of goal setting and dream chasing. No, I'm not talking about your dreams of dating that cute TikTok star (though, hey, that could be one). Instead, we're focusing on your grand ambitions, the kind that make your heart pound with excitement and a bit of fear.

Who Run the World? Girls with Goals!

You've probably heard that you need goals, right? Something about keeping us focused, blah, blah, blah. Well, I'm here to tell you that setting goals is less like your grandma's nagging and more like setting up your own personalized treasure hunt, where X marks the spot of your wildest dreams.

Chasing Dreams, Not Clouds

"Wait a minute," I hear you say, "What's the difference between a dream and a goal?" Well, think of a dream as a beautiful cloud in the sky, it's nice to look at, but it's out of reach. A goal, on the other hand, is like a ladder leading to that cloud. Each rung is a step you take to reach your dream. Your dreams may seem lofty, but your goals are the stepping stones that will get you there.

You've Got This, Darling!

So, let's put our dream-chasing hats on, shall we? What's that dream of yours? Want to become a bestselling author? A successful entrepreneur? Or maybe, save the world one recyclable straw at a time? Whatever it is, no dream is too big or too small. It's yours, and it's worth chasing.

A Goal Without a Plan is Just a Wish

Let's turn your dreams into goals with some serious action-planning. Break down your lofty dreams into manageable goals. Let's say you want to become a bestselling author. Your goals could be as simple as "Write for 20 minutes each day" or "Finish a chapter by the end of the week." Each completed goal is a victorious step closer to your dream.

Celebrate Your Victories

No victory is too small to celebrate. Did you write for 20 minutes today? Time to break out the confetti! When you recognize and celebrate your progress, you're telling yourself, "I'm on the right path. I can do this." And trust me, you can!

Riding the Roller Coaster

Remember, the journey towards your dreams may feel like a roller coaster ride. There will be highs, lows, and maybe some unexpected loops. Embrace them all. Every twist and turn is adding to your life's amazing adventure story. The fear is real, but hey, so is the fun!

A Little Help From Your Friends

Don't forget to share your journey with others. Create a dream-chasing squad with your friends. Share your goals, celebrate each other's victories, and support each other when things get tough. There's strength in numbers, and together, you can move mountains!

So, my aspiring dream chasers, remember, your dreams are the wings that let your spirit soar. Your goals are the wind beneath those wings. So let's set some goals, dream big, and make those dreams your reality. After all, the world is waiting to see the magic you're going to create!

Exploring Your Strengths and Weaknesses: Understanding Your Potential

Alright, missy! We're going on a little safari. No, not the jungle-filled, Lion King kind of safari. I'm talking about a safari of self-discovery, where we're tracking down our strengths and weaknesses. Don't worry, there won't be any big scary animals - unless you count that monstrous habit of procrastination!

Let's Get S.W.O.T-ified!

You might be thinking, "Wait, I thought SWOT was just for businesses." And you're right, but your life isn't that different from a business, think about it. You have goals (profits), obstacles (competitors), and resources (assets). A SWOT analysis is a great tool to understand our Strengths, Weaknesses, Opportunities, and Threats. But for now, we'll focus on the first two.

Flexing Your Strengths

Let's start with strengths, and no, I'm not talking about how many shopping bags you can carry at once (though, let's be real, that's a serious talent). Your strengths are the things you're naturally good at. Maybe you've got a way with words, or perhaps you're that person who can smooth over any conflict with a smile and a few kind words. Whatever your strengths are, they're your superpowers. Own them!

Weaknesses: More like Fun-sized Opportunities!

Next, weaknesses, which we're going to rename "fun-sized opportunities." Why? Because weaknesses aren't permanent. With a little elbow grease and a dash of perseverance, they can become strengths. Maybe you're a chronic procrastinator, or you have a hard time speaking up in class. That's okay. The first step in conquering our weaknesses is acknowledging them.

Dear Diary, It's SWOT Time

To identify your strengths and weaknesses, it might be helpful to keep a "SWOT diary." Take a few minutes each day to jot down when you felt at your best (hello, strengths!) and when you felt challenged (nice to meet you, weaknesses). Over time, you'll start to see patterns that can help you understand yourself better.

Strengths and Weaknesses Besties

Here's the fun part, your strengths and weaknesses are actually best friends. They work together to make you, well, you. Maybe you're incredibly creative (strength) but struggle with staying organized (weakness). That's alright. It's all about balance.

You vs. You: The Epic Battle

Remember, this journey of exploring strengths and weaknesses isn't about comparing yourself to others. You're not in a race against your best friend, the Instagram influencer, or your older sibling who got straight A's. This is your journey, your battle. And guess what? You're winning.

Lean on Me

Don't forget you're not alone on this journey. Lean on your support system - friends, family, mentors, or your pet iguana, if that's your thing. They can offer insight and encouragement as you venture into your self-exploration safari.

I'm Still Standing

Lastly, remember to celebrate how far you've come. Each day, you're learning, growing, and becoming a little more "you." That's something to be proud of. So give yourself a high-five, a pat on the back, or better yet, a full-blown dance party.

So, fasten your safari hats, take a deep breath, buckle up, and step into the wild lands of self-discovery. This is your adventure, your journey, your potential waiting to be unleashed. Let's dive in and get to know the fabulous you a little better!

Facing Fears:
Stepping Out of Your Comfort Zone

Oh, comfort zones, those cozy, cushiony spaces where everything is familiar and nothing ever surprises us. Imagine them as bubble-wrapped worlds, where we're bundled up in the warm blanket of routine, free from fear and discomfort. Sounds pretty nice, right? Well, there's a catch! Staying within this bubble-wrapped world often means that we don't grow, we don't learn, and we don't experience the full technicolor wonder of life.

Jump into the Great Unknown

Let's get this straight: comfort zones are like those super fluffy, cloud-like marshmallows. They're soft, sweet, and super easy to sink into. But have you ever tried to build anything out of marshmallows? Exactly, it's nearly impossible. To build, create, and grow, we need to step into the unknown - that scary place outside of the marshmallow. And that means facing our fears.

Fear, the Friend You Never Knew You Had

Now, fear can be an overwhelming and paralyzing emotion, it's true. But it can also be an incredibly powerful motivator and guide. Fear often pops up when we're about to do something significant or transformative. It's like that annoying alarm clock that goes off way too early in the morning; it's trying to wake us up to a new day, a new experience, a new adventure.

Dance With the Fear

So how do you go about facing these fears? You dance with them. No, seriously, it's like learning a new dance. At first, you're going to step on some toes, maybe trip a little, but with practice, you'll find your rhythm. So next time fear decides to cut in, don't sit out the dance, take the lead and show fear your moves!

The Art of Fear-Chasing

Chasing after what scares you might sound like the plot of a horror movie, but it's actually the key to unlocking your potential. Do something that scares you, and I promise, you'll feel like a superhero afterwards.

You're probably thinking, "Okay, so I just jump off a cliff or something, right?" Well, not exactly. It's all about baby steps. You don't need to go skydiving tomorrow (unless that's on your bucket list!). Start small. Speak up in class, try a new activity, ask that cutie from third period out. Whatever scares you, take a deep breath, and tackle it head-on.

Mementos of Bravery

Facing your fears is a brave act, and brave acts should be celebrated. After each fear-facing activity, reward yourself. It could be a sweet treat, a self-care day, or simply a pat on the back. You might even consider creating a "bravery jar," where you drop a note each time you face a fear. When you're feeling particularly scared or unsure, open up the jar and remind yourself of all the times you've been brave before. It's like carrying around your very own cheering squad.

Embrace the Beautiful Oops

Remember, it's okay to stumble, to fumble, and to fall flat on your face. In fact, it's more than okay; it's a beautiful oops. Each stumble is a learning opportunity, each fumble a chance to get better, each fall a lesson in getting back up. So, laugh at the missteps, learn from the trips, and remember, each time you get back up, you're a little stronger than before.

The Extraordinary Outside

Just outside of your comfort zone, there's a whole world of experiences waiting for you. It's a place where fear turns into courage, where uncertainty transforms into exploration, and where the ordinary morphs into the extraordinary. So, take that leap, make that move, and step outside. After all, the only thing scarier than facing your fears is missing out on the incredible journey they can take you on. Let's chase those fears together and uncover the incredible potential that's been within you all along

Self-Reflection and Growth: The Power of Personal Development

Close your eyes and imagine you're a plot of land. Stick with me, here. Okay, so you're a plot of land. Now, without taking care of this land, without watering it, providing it with nutrients, and nurturing it, nothing will grow. But with a little love, a little care, and a little time, that once barren plot of land can blossom into a beautiful, thriving garden. This, my friends, is the power of personal development.

Becoming a Self-Gardener

Now, before you start looking for a green thumb, let me explain. Personal development is about tending to your internal garden, cultivating your talents, growing your strengths, and trimming back your weaknesses. It's about making sure you are in full bloom. And, just like gardening, personal development starts with understanding what you're working with.

Digging Deeper

To nurture your inner garden, you first need to dig deep. This involves self-reflection, a crucial part of personal growth. Reflection allows us to understand our thoughts, feelings, and actions. It's like looking at your reflection in a pool of water. If the water is still, you can see clearly. But if the water is rippling or disturbed, it's hard to make out what you see. By taking the time to reflect, you're allowing the water to become still, providing you with a clear view of your true self.

The Power of a Thought Diary

Ever considered keeping a thought diary? Don't worry; this isn't about detailing your every thought about that cutie in your math class or the new season of your favorite Netflix show. A thought diary is a place to jot down your thoughts, feelings, and experiences on a regular basis. It's like having a conversation with yourself. With time, you'll start seeing patterns and gaining insights about yourself. Think of it as a map leading you to hidden treasure – you!

Harvesting the Fruits of Reflection

Reflection can sometimes feel a bit like staring into a mirror and seeing a pimple right on your nose. It's a bit uncomfortable, sometimes even embarrassing, but it's the first step to clearing up your skin. Reflection helps you identify your areas of growth – your pimples, if you will. Once you identify these, you can start applying metaphorical acne cream in the form of self-improvement practices. And voila! Over time, you'll start seeing changes, growth, and yes, the beautiful skin underneath.

Growing Pains and Blooming Gains

Now, let me be clear: self-reflection and growth aren't always easy. In fact, they often come with their fair share of growing pains. But just as a caterpillar must endure the confinement of its chrysalis before emerging as a butterfly, we too must go through challenges to reach our full potential.

Living Room Dance Parties and Other Growth Opportunities

Remember, growth doesn't always have to be serious. It can be as simple as trying a new type of dance in your living room, learning to cook a challenging recipe, or even just saying "yes" to an opportunity that scares you. Each new experience, each step out of your comfort zone, each living room dance party is a chance for you to grow and flourish.

Unleashing Your Blooming Self

Personal development and self-growth are like flowers blooming; they're a beautiful, gradual, and rewarding process. By dedicating time to self-reflection and self-improvement, you're investing in the most important person in your life - you. So, go ahead, nurture your inner garden, and watch as you grow into the most vibrant, most incredible, and most powerful version of you. After all, the world needs more blooming gardens, and your time to blossom is right now.

Finding Your Purpose:
Aligning Your Passions with a Meaningful Path

Have you ever played the game of connect the dots? Where you draw lines from one number to the next, and slowly but surely, a picture begins to emerge? Think of your purpose as the picture that is waiting to be revealed, with your passions being the individual dots you're connecting.

But hold on a minute - how do we even begin to discover our purpose? It's not like it's going to fall from the sky with a tag attached saying, "Here I am, your purpose! Found me yet?" Or is it?

Well, there's no magic formula to finding your purpose (sorry, Hogwarts fans!), but there are ways you can start figuring it out.

Sparks of Passion

Firstly, think about what lights you up, what brings that twinkle to your eyes and that spring in your step. It could be anything, from painting murals to solving algebraic equations (yes, for some people, math can indeed be a passion, believe it or not). Your passions are clues leading you towards your purpose.

The Power of Whys

Once you've identified your passions, start asking "Why?" Why does painting make you feel alive? Why does solving math problems give you a rush? The answers to these questions might reveal deeper layers of your passions and guide you closer to your purpose.

The Intersection of Joy and Impact

Finding your purpose often involves figuring out how you can make a positive impact on the world while doing something you love. It's like finding that sweet spot where your joy meets the world's needs. For instance, if you love painting and believe in the power of art to inspire and heal, maybe your purpose involves using your art to help others in some way.

Experiment, Explore, Evolve

Discovering your purpose isn't a one-time event. It's a journey of exploration and evolution. So, give yourself the freedom to try new things, to follow your curiosities, to make glorious mistakes and to learn from them. Maybe you'll try salsa dancing and find that it's not your thing, or maybe you'll write a poem one day and realize it's a form of expression you've been craving.

Remember, it's okay not to have everything figured out yet. Heck, even adults twice your age are still figuring things out! What matters is that you're taking steps towards discovering your purpose, no matter how small or uncertain those steps might be.

Not All Those Who Wander Are Lost

J.R.R. Tolkien got it right with this one. Wandering, exploring, questioning - these are not signs of being lost, but signs of being on the path to finding your purpose. So, put on your explorer hat, get out your metaphorical compass, and start navigating the vast landscape of your passions and potentials. Who knows what exciting, purpose-filled destinations await you!

At the end of the day, your purpose isn't something you find hiding under a rock. It's something you reveal by connecting the dots of your passions, by daring to ask why, and by having the courage to wander, explore, and grow. So, what are you waiting for? Your meaningful path is waiting to be discovered, and only you can uncover it.

Chapter 18:

Cultivating Resilience: Bouncing Back from Life's Challenges

The Power of Resilience: Building Inner Strength

Okay, picture this: you're in a bouncy castle (c'mon, age is just a number, right?). You're having the time of your life, jumping, flipping, and rolling around. But every now and then, a wild jump sends you crashing into the castle's inflatable walls. What happens? You bounce back, right? You don't stay smushed against the wall. You don't sink to the floor in defeat. Nope, you bounce back, ready for the next jump, the next flip, the next roll.

That, my friend, is a fun, colorful, and slightly goofy metaphor for resilience.

Resilience isn't about never falling down or never facing challenges; it's about bouncing back each time we do. It's that little voice in our heads that whispers, "You got this," when we're knee-deep in challenges. It's the strength that helps us stand up after we've been knocked down and whispers in our ears, "You're more powerful than this setback. Show it who's boss."

So, how do you build this sort of inner strength? Here are a few nuggets of wisdom to get you started:

Friendship with Failure

First, you've got to become friends with failure. Wait, what?! Become friends with failure? Yes, you read that right. See, failure often gets a bad rap, but it's actually one of the most effective teachers you'll ever meet. Every time you fail, you learn what doesn't work, which means you're one step closer to finding what does. So, don't be scared to fail. Embrace it, learn from it, and let it fuel your resilience.

Self-Talk Matters

Next, pay attention to how you talk to yourself. If you constantly tell yourself things like, "I can't handle this," or "I'm not strong enough," then guess what? You're going to start believing it. But if you tell yourself, "I can handle this," or "I am strong," you'll start to believe that instead. The words you tell yourself shape your reality, so make sure they're words of resilience and strength.

Support Squad

Remember, building resilience doesn't mean you have to face everything alone. In fact, having a support squad can do wonders for your resilience. This squad could be friends, family, a counselor, or even online communities of people facing similar challenges. When you have others cheering you on, it's easier to bounce back from life's bouncy castle moments.

Gratitude Attitude

Even in the midst of challenges, there's always something to be grateful for. Maybe it's a hot cup of tea on a cold morning, a text from a friend, or simply the fact that you're alive and breathing.

Cultivating an attitude of gratitude helps you focus on the positives, making it easier to bounce back from the negatives.

Keep Going

Finally, remember this: resilience is a journey, not a destination. There will be days when you'll bounce back like a pro, and there will be days when it will take all your strength just to get back up. That's okay. What matters is that you keep going, keep bouncing back, keep building your inner strength.

So, the next time life sends you crashing into the inflatable walls of your bouncy castle, remember: you're not defeated. You're just gathering momentum for your next bounce. After all, you're stronger than you think, and your bounce-back power is just waiting to be unleashed.

Coping with Failure and Rejection: Turning Setbacks into Opportunities

Alright, grab your comfort snacks and let's get real for a moment. If I had a dollar for every time I've failed or faced rejection, I could probably buy out a whole Sephora store (or at least a few high-end palettes, am I right?). Whether it's a bad grade on a test, a breakup, a job rejection, or a negative comment on your latest TikTok dance (yes, even that counts), failure and rejection are just part and parcel of this wild ride called life.

But here's the plot twist: failure and rejection aren't the evil villains they're made out to be. Nope, they're more like those misunderstood characters in movies who seem all gruff and mean on the outside, but have a heart of gold deep down. You just need to know how to approach them. So, grab your metaphorical popcorn and let's dive in.

Setback or Setup?

First, let's tackle the mind-bender: is it a setback or a setup for a comeback? Take a moment to think about the times when you failed or faced rejection. I know, it's like voluntarily walking into a haunted house, but trust me on this. Look beyond the disappointment and embarrassment, and you'll often find valuable lessons and opportunities for growth.

Maybe that failed test showed you that pulling all-nighters isn't your best study strategy. Or maybe that job rejection led you to an even better opportunity you wouldn't have found otherwise. So, the next time you face a setback, ask yourself: "What can I learn from this? How can this help me grow?"

Give Yourself Permission to Feel

We've all heard the saying, "Don't cry over spilled milk." But what if that milk was part of your perfect morning latte, and you're now late for school with no coffee in hand? Feeling disappointed, sad, or frustrated is perfectly normal. Allow yourself to experience these emotions without judgment. They validate your experience and help you process what happened. So, go ahead, have a mini pity party if you need to. Just don't forget to pack up the streamers and get back to the grind when it's over.

The Power of Perspective

Remember when you used to think that the cooties were the worst thing ever? And look at you now, swiping right and left on dating apps like a pro. Perspective changes everything. When faced with failure or rejection, widen your perspective and see the bigger picture. One rejection or failure doesn't define you or your abilities. It's just a single brushstroke on the vast canvas of your life.

Celebrate the Brave

Even in the face of failure or rejection, don't forget to celebrate the fact that you tried. You put yourself out there. You took a risk. You were brave. And that's worth celebrating. So, go ahead and treat yourself to a spa day, a movie night, or that lipstick you've been eyeing for weeks. You deserve it.

Keep Moving Forward

Finally, just keep swimming. It's okay if you need a life vest (aka a good cry or a pep talk from a friend) from time to time. What matters is that you keep moving forward. Every step, no matter how small, is progress.

So, the next time failure or rejection knocks on your door, welcome them in with a sly grin. Because now you know their secret: they're not here to break you, but to shape you. They're not roadblocks, but stepping stones to your amazing future. And that's the kind of plot twist that makes for a fantastic story. So, keep writing your story, one brave, resilience-building chapter at a time.

Mindset Shift:
Embracing a Positive Attitude

Alright, grab your unicorn slippers and your fairy lights because we're about to embark on a magical journey into the realm of mindset shifts and positive attitudes. "But wait," I hear you groan, "Isn't that just some fancy term for seeing the glass as half full?" Yes and no, dear reader. It's more like seeing the glass as refillable. But let's not get ahead of ourselves. Time to buckle up, sprinkle some positivity dust, and let's dive right in.

Positivity Isn't Denying Reality

First things first, let's get one thing clear: being positive doesn't mean denying reality or pretending everything is fine when it's not. That's like trying to stick a band-aid on a broken arm and expecting it to heal. Positivity is about acknowledging the good in every situation, even when things seem as chaotic as your bedroom during exam week.

The Magic of Perception

Your world is shaped by your perception. Ever notice how when you buy a new pair of shoes, suddenly you start seeing them everywhere? That's your perception at play. The same goes for positivity. If you constantly focus on the negatives, the world can seem as gloomy as a vampire movie. But when you shift your mindset to focus on the positives, suddenly the world shines brighter than your highlighter on a Saturday night.

Positivity Is an Inside Job

Just like the perfect winged eyeliner, positivity comes from within. It's an inside job. It's about empowering yourself to see the good, even in the most challenging situations. When you've studied for hours and still can't remember the difference between mitosis and meiosis, remember to appreciate your determination and commitment. That's positivity in action.

Your Thoughts Are Powerful

Your thoughts are like those gossipy friends who can't keep a secret. Whatever you think, your mind believes. Ever had that moment where you kept telling yourself you'd fail a test, and then you did? That's because your thoughts shape your beliefs, and your beliefs shape your actions. So, if you tell yourself that you're capable, strong, and resilient, your actions will reflect that. Remember, you're the queen of your mental castle. Choose your thoughts wisely.

The Positivity Potion

Okay, I can't give you a magic potion that will instantly make you positive (trust me, if I had one, I'd be bottling it up and selling it). But I can give you some ingredients to brew your own positivity potion.

Gratitude: Being grateful is like adding glitter to any situation. It immediately makes things better. Try keeping a gratitude journal where you jot down three things you're grateful for each day. It could be as simple as a good hair day or as big as acing your finals.

Self-Love: This is the cherry on top of your positivity potion. Be kind to yourself. Treat yourself as you would your best friend. Encourage yourself, pamper yourself, and most importantly, forgive yourself. Perfection is overrated anyway.

Mindfulness: Living in the moment is like sipping your favorite latte. It's calming, soothing, and brings instant joy. Try to stay present and savor each moment instead of constantly worrying about the future or dwelling on the past.

So, the next time you find yourself sliding into a pit of negativity, remember to dust off your unicorn slippers, light up your fairy lights, and brew yourself a batch of positivity potion. Remember, no matter how the world looks, you have the power to add a dash of glitter and make it shine. Your positivity is your magic wand, and with it, you can transform your world.

Managing Stress and Overwhelm: Strategies for Well-being

Hey there, beautiful! Let's talk about something that's probably as constant in your life as your 24/7 love for pizza and Netflix: stress and overwhelm. Just like that one annoying classmate who won't stop texting you, stress and overwhelm often overstay their welcome. But it's time to turn the tables and gain control. So, grab your favorite blanket, whip up a cup of soothing chamomile tea, and let's dive into some stress-busting secrets.

Stress: A Wolf in Sheep's Clothing

We often treat stress like that rogue pimple that just won't quit. We pretend it's not there, or we cover it up with concealer, hoping it will magically disappear. But just like that stubborn pimple, stress has a knack for popping up when we least expect it. The reality is, stress is a normal part of life, and it's not all bad. In small doses, it can motivate us to ace that test or perfect that dance routine. But when it starts taking over your life, making you feel like you're juggling five flaming torches while riding a unicycle, it's time to take action.

Understanding Overwhelm

Overwhelm is like stress's annoying little sibling. It often shows up when there's too much on your plate—too many tasks, too many expectations, too many choices. You know that feeling when you have a project due tomorrow, two tests next week, and no idea what to wear to the party on Saturday? That's overwhelm knocking at your door.

Stress and Overwhelm, Meet Self-Care

Self-care is your superhero when it comes to fighting stress and overwhelm. And no, self-care isn't just about bubble baths and face masks (although those are great, too). Self-care is about taking time to nurture your body, mind, and spirit. It's about setting boundaries, prioritizing your needs, and saying "no" when you need to.

But let's break down self-care into bite-sized pieces:

Physical self-care: This includes regular exercise (dance parties in your room totally count), balanced nutrition (yes, veggies and fruits are still in), and adequate sleep (you're not a vampire, you need your beauty sleep).

Emotional self-care: Allow yourself to feel your emotions without judgment. It's okay to cry when you're sad, and it's okay to scream into a pillow when you're angry. Emotional self-care also means seeking support when needed. Talking to a trusted friend, family member, or mental health professional can provide emotional relief.

Spiritual self-care: This is all about connecting with your inner self and finding meaning in your life. It can involve meditation, yoga, spending time in nature, or practicing mindfulness. It's all about what makes your soul feel peaceful and content.

The Power of Breath

One of the quickest and most effective ways to combat stress and overwhelm is by harnessing the power of your breath. Deep, slow breathing can help to slow your heart rate and relax your muscles, providing a calming effect. You can try different breathing techniques like the 4-7-8 breathing technique (inhale for 4 seconds, hold for 7, exhale for 8) or belly breathing. Yes, it sounds super simple, but it's like a secret weapon against stress. Give it a try next time you're feeling overwhelmed.

Reframe Your Thoughts

Our thoughts can often fuel stress and overwhelm. For example, thinking "I have to get an A on this test, or I'm a failure" is going to cause a lot more stress than thinking "I'll do my best on this test, but my worth isn't defined by a grade." Try to catch yourself when you're slipping into negative thought patterns and reframe them into something more positive and supportive.

Remember, lovely girl, stress and overwhelm may be a part of life, but they don't have to run the show. You have the tools to manage them and the strength to overcome them. You're resilient, you're powerful, and you've got this. Now, go on and show stress and overwhelm who's boss! And always remember to take a deep breath, unwind with your favorite activity, and keep your self-care game strong. Here's to a calmer, happier you!

Building a Support System: Nurturing Healthy Relationships

We're opening the book on one of the most important elements of resilience: your support system. It's time to delve into the amazing world of relationships and how they impact our resilience. I'm not just talking about the 'we-watched-the-sunrise-together' kind of relationships, but all sorts of connections in our lives. So, buckle up, grab your fuzziest socks, and get ready for this fabulous journey into the realm of relationships!

First thing's first, let's understand what a 'support system' means. It's not a fancy new app on your phone or some scientific term you need to memorize. It's simply a network of people who provide you with practical or emotional support. They are the ones who stand by you in times of trouble and join you in a happy dance when you pass that ridiculously tough chemistry test.

Your support system can include anyone: friends, family, teachers, mentors, or even your grumpy but surprisingly wise next-door neighbor. These are the people who make up your personal cheerleading squad, those who lift you up, believe in you, and add that extra sparkle to your life.

Friends: The Family You Choose

Good friends are like your favorite pair of jeans: reliable, comfortable, and they make you feel amazing! These are the people who share your laughter, tears, and countless pizza slices at 2 am. They're there to offer a shoulder to cry on, a much-needed reality check, or a fierce 'you-go-girl' pep talk. Remember, quality trumps quantity every time when it comes to friends. It's better to have a few close friends who truly have your back than a thousand 'friends' who disappear at the first sign of trouble.

Family: The OG Support System

Families are like those embarrassing childhood photos your parents insist on showing everyone—they can be a little awkward at times, but they're also an undeniable part of you. Your family knows you at your best and your worst, and they still love you anyway. They provide a safe harbor in the stormy seas of life. And if you're lucky enough to have siblings, you know they can be your fiercest rivals and your most steadfast allies.

Mentors: Your Personal Yoda

A mentor is someone who has walked the path before you, gained wisdom and experience, and is willing to guide you on your journey. They could be a teacher, a coach, or even a family friend. They're there to inspire you, to share their wisdom, and to help you navigate the complex maze of life.

Creating and Maintaining Your Support System

Building a solid support system doesn't happen overnight. It requires time, effort, and loads of patience. Here are a few tips:

Be open: Don't be afraid to express yourself. Vulnerability may seem scary, but it's the key to building deep, meaningful connections.

Give and take: Relationships are a two-way street. Be there for others, just as they are there for you. Listen to their problems, celebrate their wins, and offer help when they need it.

Quality over quantity: You don't need a big crowd. A few solid, trustworthy relationships can make a world of difference.

Nurture your relationships: Like plants, relationships need to be nurtured to grow. Regular 'watering' with love, respect, and care can go a long way.

Know when to let go: Not all relationships are meant to last forever, and that's okay. If a relationship is causing you more pain than joy, it might be time to say goodbye. Your well-being should always come first.

Remember, ladies, your support system is your emotional safety net, your cheerleading squad, and your personal superheroes all rolled into one. They might not be perfect, but they are the ones who'll stand by you through thick and thin. So, appreciate them, cherish them, and most importantly, don't forget to return the favor! Here's to building strong, healthy, and empowering relationships in your life!

Thriving Through Adversity: Embracing Change and Adaptability

As we continue to navigate the twists and turns of resilience, it's time to look adversity in the eye and say, "Bring it on!" Today, we are focusing on a superpower we all possess but often overlook – the power to thrive through adversity. Yes, you heard right. We're going to dive into the glorious messiness of change and adaptability. So, prepare to unleash your inner resilience rockstar, because this is going to be a wild ride!

Let's get real for a second. Life can be as unpredictable as a zebra on a rollercoaster (yeah, try visualizing that!). Just when you think you've got it all figured out, BAM! You're hit with a curveball. Your once comfy and predictable life is suddenly in a whirlwind of change, and you're left feeling like a fish out of water.

Now, I know what you're thinking, "Great, just what I needed! More chaos!" But wait, hold onto your unicorn socks because there's a silver lining to this storm cloud. This change, this adversity, it's not your enemy. It's actually a golden ticket to discover just how truly resilient you are.

The Tumble Dry Cycle of Life

Picture this: life's like a gigantic tumble dryer. We all go in as wrinkled pieces of clothing, and the dryer's job is to shake us, spin us around, and eventually, smooth out our wrinkles. Sounds fun, right? Okay, maybe not. But it's in this chaotic spinning that we grow, we adapt, and we come out stronger, smoother, and more resilient.

Embrace the Change

Change is as inevitable as the latest fashion trend (who knew scrunchies would make such a big comeback, right?). It's the only constant in life. So, instead of resisting it, let's embrace it. When you do, you'll find that change isn't some big, scary monster. Instead, it's an opportunity to learn, to grow, and to discover new paths.

Unleash Your Adaptability Superpower

Now, onto the A-word: adaptability. This is the ability to adjust to new conditions, to roll with the punches, to pick yourself up after a setback, dust off your fabulous self, and say, "What's next?" It's about learning to dance in the rain, even when you've forgotten your umbrella. It's the secret sauce to thriving through adversity.

Thriving, Not Just Surviving

Surviving is just getting by, like floating on a raft in the middle of the ocean. Thriving, on the other hand, is about learning to ride the waves, using the wind to steer you forward, and finding joy in the journey. It's about making the most of every situation, even the tough ones.

So, how do you shift from just surviving to absolutely thriving?

Embrace a growth mindset: View challenges as opportunities to learn and grow, not as insurmountable obstacles. Your mindset is a powerful tool. Use it wisely.

Practice gratitude: Even in the worst of times, there's always something to be grateful for. Find it. Cherish it. Let it be the beacon of light in your storm.

Stay flexible: Be like a palm tree, which bends in the storm but doesn't break. Be open to new ideas, perspectives, and solutions.

Nurture your physical and mental health: Exercise regularly, eat healthily, sleep well, and practice mindfulness. A healthy body and mind make you better equipped to face adversity.

Maintain your support system: Remember, it's okay to lean on others for support. You don't have to face adversity alone. Reach out to your support system, and let them help you navigate through the tough times.

Remember, thriving through adversity isn't about avoiding challenges or pretending they don't exist. It's about facing them head-on, harnessing your inner strength, and coming out on the other side stronger, wiser, and more resilient.

So here's to embracing change, unleashing your adaptability superpower, and thriving through adversity. You've got this, superstar! Let's rock this rollercoaster of life together!

Conclusion

Wow, look at you, rockstar! You've come a long way, haven't you? You've plunged into the deep end of adulthood and swum through the tidal waves of change, friendships, love, health, money matters, and so much more. Who would've thought that we'd even survive through chapters on marriage and voting, let alone mental health and career planning? But look at us now – we did it, and girl, I couldn't be prouder!

If this book were a Spotify playlist, it'd be one crazy mix of pop, rock, country, and probably a bit of 90's boy band nostalgia. But that's the beauty of it – our journey through adulthood isn't meant to be a monotonous tune. It's meant to be a blend of different genres, sometimes a soulful ballad, other times a rock anthem, but each one a hit in its own right.

And you, my dear, are the lead vocalist, the one who sets the rhythm of your life. This book was never meant to be a rulebook, but more like a collection of mixtapes from your best friend – full of advice, shared experiences, love, and a few cheesy jokes.

Remember, this journey we embarked on wasn't about becoming someone else. It was about discovering who you truly are. It's about finding your voice amidst the noise, learning to embrace your beautifully unique self, and dancing to your own rhythm.

Through each chapter, we've discovered that life's complexities and curveballs are not monsters under the bed, but rather stepping stones to our growth. We learned that it's okay to laugh, cry, love, break, and rebuild. We've talked about our bodies, our minds, our hearts, and our spirits. We've explored every nook and cranny of what it means to be 18, to be an adult, to be a human, to be YOU.

And oh, what a marvelous, messy, and magical journey it has been! Just like Taylor Swift's discography, our journey had its "Love Story" moments and its "Bad Blood" days. But no matter the song, remember that it's all part of your story, your album.

Let's not forget the strength we discovered within us, the resilience we nurtured, the dragons we slayed. The "Self-Exploration" and "Cultivating Resilience" chapters didn't just remind us of our true potential and inner strength but showed us that we are unstoppable, even when we feel like we're falling apart.

Remember, no amount of change, stress, or failure can take away your power to adapt and thrive. Because darling, you're not just a star, you're a whole galaxy!

Finally, let's talk about one more thing – this isn't the end. Yes, you heard that right. Just as the end of one song is the beginning of another, this isn't the end of our journey. It's just the start of a new chapter. A chapter written and directed by you. A chapter where you're the heroine of your own story. A chapter full of adventures waiting to be embarked on.

So go on, girl. Lace up your combat boots, put on your sparkly unicorn socks, wear your heart on your sleeve, and step into the world with your head held high. Life's a wild ride, and we're all here for it. So let's make it a good one, shall we?

With that, it's time for me to sign off, but not without one final toast – Here's to the tears, the laughter, the lessons, and the journey. Here's to the girl you were, the woman you're becoming, and the incredible story you're writing.

Here's to you, rockstar. Let the adventure continue. You've got this!